Kingdom Chronicles

True Tales of Guts, Glory, and Spiritual Authority

Kingdom Chronicles:

True Tales of Guts, Glory, and Spiritual Authority

Chronicle: a factual account of important events

Then those who feared the Lord spoke to one another, and the Lord listened and heard them; so a book of remembrance was written before Him.

(Malachi 3:16 NKJV)

Often we judge someone's life from an external perspective. In other words, from what we see. Such a limiting view! So much more is unfolding within every single person, in their heart of hearts. Joy, sorrow, trouble, excitement, breakthrough; all kinds of experiences, emotions, reactions, breakthroughs. Both spiritual and natural. Spirit, soul, body. These vignettes paint a broad spectrum of life experiences, God adventures. They speak faith, risk, God's goodness, faithfulness, mans perseverance, endurance, even fun! Take this book, read a chapter a day, a chapter a week. Ponder what is being said and let it speak into your life and bring you hope, courage and even fun! Testimonies are prophetic declarations shouting out, do it again Lord in my life!

- Barbara Yoder, Shekinah Church, Ann Arbor Michigan

Kingdom Chronicles is an extraordinary book filled with stories from an exceptional group of Godly women! Many of the authors I have known for years, through our annual Women In Strategic Leadership roundtables. Their tales of adventures with God as they advance His Kingdom will amuse you, encourage you, and stir you to action. it is easy to read, but it will challenge you to the core. I highly recommend Kingdom Chronicles. It is a book that should be on the reading list of every Christian leader.

- Dr. Rev. Diane Wigstone - Director YWAMHollywood.com, President DestinyCenter.com, Speaker, & Author

The collective journeys of these fourteen powerful women of fire will dig your spiritual well deeper. Together they have the wisdom of a pastor, the heart of an evangelist, the fire of a revivalist, and the boldness of a prophet. Let their guts, glory, and spiritual authority stories spur you on to a greater works ministry in life and leadership!

- Dr. Jamie Morgan - Author of Thirsty, a 31-day journey to personal revival

Fantastic, compelling, real-life stories that will strengthen your faith so you will rise up and overcome every challenge that invades your life. These writers have been there, done this—proving God is faithful. You can hear the cry of their heart: Don't give up—press forward into God's promises.

The kingdom takeaways at the end of each story are fantastic guides that will enable you to apply each encounter in your own life. This book is great for personal as well as group discussions and victorious prayers. Buy this and share it with others. You will never be the same!

- Rev. Dr. Naomi Dowdy - Founder Chancellor, TCA College Singapore, Former Senior Pastor, Trinity Christian Centre, Singapore, Speaker, Author, Mentor, Trainer, Consultant

True Tales

Thank you to Terry Murphy for her labor of love reading and rereading our stories with gracious suggestions for our content flow.

Foreword

By JoAnne Meckstroth

My daughter Dianne and I often use each other as sounding boards, particularly when exploring an interesting foundational principle or kingdom concept. She also knows many of the women who participated in this book. When she joined me in my study, I told her I was gathering a few thoughts for the foreword I'd been asked to write for the stories you're about to read. She laughed out loud before sharing this vision the Lord had given her.

> "I see angels sitting in the rafters, their legs swinging as they hang over the beam. They are casually talking with each other. One comments to his neighbor, 'You're looking fit, what's your secret?'
>
> "His angelic buddy flexes his arm, sword in hand. 'I love this assignment! Reminds me of when we joined God's heavenly host and had all that grueling combat training with Michael—never a dull moment with this one!'
>
> "The third angel laughs. 'Me too. Remember when we would wait around for days or even weeks for something to happen? I thought about asking to be assigned to someone else. Not anymore!" They all laugh, their swords clanking against the beams as they continue swinging their legs."

The angels on assignment in this vision are symbolic of God's heavenly host assigned to come alongside us. They're battling in the spirit realm as we boldly go about God's kingdom business here on earth and take back the ground the enemy has stolen.

The stories of these fourteen women illustrate how our lives can be full enough to keep even those angels assigned to us interested and excited. You'll find these disarmingly simple chapters deeply moving. They'll show you how you, too, can learn to live, lead and establish God's kingdom in the midst of a dark and unbelieving society.

Having the angelic host on standby to fight the enemy in the spiritual realm was certainly indispensable for the women joining together on this project.

But they'd all agree the greatest gift by far they've ever received was the Holy Spirit Himself. Out of this vital relationship came a supernatural invasion of His presence, His intimacy and His power. With Him came a zeal and boldness to fight their daily battles and win.

In Matthew 11:12, during a discourse about John the Baptist, Jesus made a strange statement. "And from the days of John the Baptist until now the kingdom of heaven suffers violence and the violent take it by force," (NKJV).

The Holy Spirit, the agent of heaven, has blanketed these unique women with His supernatural power—a power that can and will invade the kingdom of darkness to destroy the works of the enemy. Like John the Baptist, these women carry what's called a "breaker anointing." For them, Matthew 11:12 contains a deeper dimension that relates to the end of the age. The constraining walls of this world must be breached for the kingdom of heaven to burst forth into the world with all the power of God.

This breaker anointing is no longer embodied in a single person as it was in John's day. It is a movement happening now—a movement that includes you.

Yes. The angels *do* have reason to be excited.

The Good in Me

By Pam Eichorn

Whatever you do, work at it with all your heart, as working for the Lord, not for men, since you know that you will receive an inheritance from the Lord as a reward. It is the Lord Christ you are serving.

(Colossians 3:23–24 NIV)

I was so excited as I read the book of stories that was a compilation of many great minds, great hearts, great women. When I came to one I had written, I was stunned. It fit in with the others.

Who would have thought I could fit in with "them?"

How often do you wonder if you measure up?

How often do you think you can, but don't?

Well, not this year, my friend. Not this year.

You have the incredible opportunity to be someone who wins, creates, becomes, leads, teaches and does.

Here is an incredible thought: Did you know that when you use God's gifts, you prove to Him that you love and worship Him?

What?

Yes! When you use the wonderful gifts inside of you—all that was placed in you at conception to be the overcomer, the victor, the leader, the full person He saw at your creation—you worship Him.

Being you is worship.

He believed in you right from the get-go, so you bring the creator God glory by being who you are. And, oh, how He loves to see His creations bring Him glory.

I am excited writing this for you, and I don't even know you. But I know my God, and if He created you, breathed into you, thought of you, then well, I have no doubt you are remarkable.

“Let us not grow weary while doing good, for in due season we shall reap if we do not lose heart,” (Galatians 6:9 NIV).

For years I thought that “good” was always doing something righteous—you know, churchy—until one day I realized something. He created the light and saw that it was good. He created the night and saw that it was good. He created man and saw that it was good. And then He saw all that He had made, and it was “very good.” (Genesis 1:4–31)

I was created “good.” So let us not grow weary of doing good because it’s being who He created us to be. The good that is in us, the gifts He gave us to use here on earth, all that is in us, all the God in us for now, is who we are to be.

We are to be us, the good in us—the writer, singer, father, mother, engineer, politician, editor, seamstress, painter, doctor, factory worker, nurse.

The good in you. The good in me.

Kingdom Takeaway

How could you better lead, be yourself and allow those you lead to be themselves?

Can you create an atmosphere where you can really hear the questions posed by those you lead? Their diversity may surprise you. Find a way to blend them into a strategy that empowers everyone on your team.

Harness the passion of your team and remain steadfast, for vision is the greatest gift of leadership. Don't give up in the days ahead. Resist draining your energy by focusing on exterior events. Rather, keep your eyes on performing the event God is stirring up within your hearts.

Finally, "Never be lacking in zeal, but keep your spiritual fervor, serving the Lord," (Romans 12:11 NIV).

The Scent of Water

By M. Janet Mangum

He who believes in Me, as the Scripture has said, out of his heart will flow rivers of living water.

(John 3:37 – 38 NKJV)

Elephants are fascinating. Whether Asian or African, they have highly developed senses that not only allow them to navigate their social and emotional world, but to find life-sustaining water. It's a critical ability because elephants need immense quantities of water—forty to sixty gallons a day.

How do they survive in a land which is commonly dry or in drought?

Coded for Life

The answer lies in divine design. Elephants are well- equipped for survival. In times of drought, they know to migrate. If a drought is severe, they travel far away, where water is more plentiful. They also know to dig into dry streambeds or other spots where water is not visible on the surface. They pound and dig with feet, trunks and tusks until an adequate supply of water appears. The amusing sight of elephants circling, stomping and digging together has been described as their dance for water.

How do they know where to dig? God has given elephants the ability to smell water (according to some reports, even at a distance of twelve or more miles). By waving their trunks in the air, they not only gather the scent of water but detect its distance and direction.

Sniffing for Living Water

Just as He did with the elephant, our Master Creator has coded within our DNA an ability to sense what will help and sustain us. Our coding, when connected with the power of the Holy Spirit, enables us to navigate the dry, dusty and irregular roads of life—showing us where and how to find His "living water."

King David expressed spiritual thirst like this in Psalm 63:1–8.

> *"You, God, are my God, earnestly I seek you; I thirst for you, my whole being longs for you, in a dry and parched land where there is no water. I have seen you in the sanctuary and beheld your power and your glory. Because your love is better than life, my lips will glorify you. I will praise you as long as I live, and in your name I will lift up my hands. I will be fully satisfied as with the richest of foods; with singing lips my mouth will praise you. On my bed I remember you; I think of you through the watches of the night. Because you are my help, I sing in the shadow of your wings. I cling to you; your right hand upholds me."* (NIV)

Our Source of Spiritual Water

Petra, Machu Picchu, or Pompeii are empty dried up ancient kingdoms. Their ruins are now only visited by curious tourists trying to imagine their previous glory. The kingdom of God, on the other hand, is a vibrant, dynamic, lifegiving reality. It flows with rivers of living water for its citizens. (Philippians 3:20, John 4:14, John 7:38)

If circumstances seem to have dried up your hope and made you feel like one of these ancient ruins, there is a refreshing well of salvation waiting to water your soul in God's kingdom. The Holy Spirit is with you to revive your spirit. He will enable you to overcome the sadness and depressing ways of the world around you. It's time to rediscover a God-given kingdom resource.

Hope for the Empty Space

My friend Gail reached the place where she said she could actually feel an empty space growing within her. "It felt dry and like something was dying inside." She couldn't put her finger on the problem.

Well-meaning friends offered her a dinner out, but their invitations held no appeal. "I didn't want to be impolite. I just wasn't interested. I was in an emotional drought. Something had drained every ounce of my desire for relational interaction. It was like being thirsty and yet not sure where to locate replenishing, clear, cool water."

Where did she look for the needful water of life? The kingdom of God. As long as this was her resource, she knew she would eventually arrive at a healthy, healing, transformative place.

Whatever "empty place" you find yourself in, you can be certain water is coming. Replenishment is not far away because the kingdom of God is near.

The Way to Water May Be Unusual

Have you ever been clueless as to how to approach someone who has suffered or is still suffering from a tragic loss? If we had met Jonah of the Bible in the middle of his losses, we likely wouldn't have known what to say to him. That's how it was when I first met Jack and Kayle.

Jack and Kayle were invited to share their personal testimony of restoration at a luncheon. They accepted because they had faced a drastic change from a tragedy. Their child had become a victim of violence and had died. It made them feel like empty, dried up, crumbling ancient ruins.

Kayle's inner being remained in extreme drought for a long time. It took years before she could speak about her experience. The day of the luncheon, she was ready to share their journey from drought to fresh-flowing living water.

Jack and Kayle began sharing their story softly and calmly. We were stunned into silence as they spoke, wondering how anyone could recover after suffering that kind of tragedy. We had no answers, no comforting thoughts or practical advice. Only God could revive such ravaged souls. His merciful, all-powerful, miraculous resurrection life was their only hope.

At the closing, I was paired with Kayle for prayer. I tentatively approached her. "I'm so stunned that you are able to speak and share with us here today."

"I couldn't do it for a long time," she said. "I was no more than an outward shell, an abandoned ruin of what once was a flourishing kingdom life. I had completely lost my way. I not only didn't know where to look, but I no longer even wanted to look for answers.

"After a while, when people came to visit trying to share their love and encouragement, I would sit and listen patiently. But it was as if nothingness had merged into nothingness. Blank. Empty. No love, no voice of encouragement penetrated. It felt as if other people were tourists visiting my dry, abandoned ruin."

Though she and Jack had been followers of Jesus before the tragedy had struck, no Scripture or Biblical promise had so far helped. "Then one day a friend came to visit," Kayle continued. "I sat dutifully listening as I always had, pretending I could hear and receive. Somewhere in the mesh of words, the visitor quoted a Scripture passage from the book of Job.

"At least there is hope for a tree: If it is cut down, it will sprout again, and its new shoots will not fail. Its roots may grow old in the ground and its stump die in the soil, yet at the scent of water it will bud and put forth shoots like a plant," (Job 14:7–9 NIV).

"From that moment on," she said, "I began to heal. It was not from the scent of water, but just from *hearing* about the scent of water from the Word of God that a tiny sprout of life began to form inside the dead tree stump I'd turned into."

As Kayle spoke, I sensed she and I were on sacred ground. Why, out of all the wonderful promises in the Bible, would this odd Scripture speak so gloriously to Kayle's inward being? Why would it cause the fresh spring of resurrection life to activate the journey toward restoration for her and her husband? To me, it was a mystery—it just didn't make sense.

Sometimes no words from others can help. Only God knows how to resurrect, restore and heal. What He uses to accomplish this can often be a complete conundrum.

The Spirit Brings Life

Just how God works His restoration miracles may remain a mystery. The fact is, He does bring hope for today. John 6:63 gives a hint in Jesus' discourse with His upset disciples. "The Spirit gives life; the flesh counts for nothing. The words I have spoken to you—they are full of the Spirit and life."

No matter what surprising way God's kingdom intervenes, when His Spirit intervenes, He brings life. We can look to the Comforter for supernatural provision when nothing, absolutely nothing, is going to bring joy out of sorrow, hope out of pain, grace out of despair, rest out of severe exhaustion and peace for the depleted soul. He may send a dream, a memory or an angelic visitation. We may hear a voice here or feel a touch there. Whether through the sound of wind or the scent of water, help is coming. The kingdom of God is here and near, and it can appear in startling ways.

Does this sound outlandish to your soul right now? That's okay.

Living Water Is Dynamic

A *dynamic* force is one that stimulates change or progress. When Jesus referred to Himself as living water, He was talking about water that is fresh and flowing. Just as rivers move rocks and change the shape of the banks, God's provision gushes forth as a dynamic for change, carving new waterways in our dry and dusty lives.

The book of John records a story of a Samaritan woman who came alone to a nearby well where Jesus was resting. As she approached, Jesus asked her to give Him a drink. She was shocked. In those days, men didn't openly speak to strange women, and Jews avoided speaking to Samaritans.

"How come you, a Jew, are asking me, a Samaritan woman, for a drink?" she asked.

Jesus answered, "If you knew the generosity of God and who I am, you would be asking me for a drink, and I would give you fresh, living water." After she questioned what He meant, Jesus continued. "Everyone who drinks this water will get thirsty again and again. Anyone who drinks the water I give will never thirst—not ever. The water I give will be an artesian spring within, gushing fountains of endless life," (John 4:7–15 MSG).

Prayer

Father God, I trust I am Your workmanship in Christ Jesus and my instincts come from Your Spirit. In time, I believe I will discover the necessary provisions, even when they are not obvious at the moment.

I believe You, Father, are activating a healthy, lifegiving transformation process from whatever stage or "dry, empty place" in which I find myself right now. In my journey of transformation, I will continue to trust Your leading. I choose to believe water is ahead. The day will come when my thirst is quenched, and my longing soul is renewed. I smile at the thought of my personal elephant dance!

Kingdom Takeaway

Everyone needs the restoration living water brings. It doesn't matter if life seems to have cut you down to the core or you feel like an old, dry riverbed lying dormant. Your spirit is on the search, sniffing the air. You may not know where to look, but your spirit will pick up the scent of water with the help of the Spirit of God.

In what ways have you made choices to remain on the journey of faith when there is no sign of desperately needed provision? How have these choices affected your sense of wellbeing?

Just as elephants smell water and begin to dance, the Spirit of God within you will lead you to His living water and your soul will dance again!

Open Door Dilemma

By Merrily Madero

"If you seek nothing but the will of God,
He will always put you in the right place at the right time."

–Smith Wigglesworth

I often hear believers say, "If the door opens, I'll know it's from the Lord and I'll go through it." I always caution them to really seek God in those situations. My experience has been that God is not the only one opening doors.

Who else might it be? The Bible tells us to be wary of Satan, whose consuming goal is to steal, kill and destroy (John 10:10). He'll influence our circumstances and try to get our eyes off God and His plan for our lives. (Satan can make his temptations appear to us like blessings.)

How do we tell which door is God's? How do we hold out for God's blessings and trust in His timing and will for our lives? By asking, listening and obeying.

Asking

I love this quote from Smith Wigglesworth: "God is more eager to answer than we are to ask." So why do we do we hesitate to ask the Lord? Maybe we think we're too busy. Maybe we assume we are already doing the right thing. But even if something lines up with the Word of God, it may not be in His timing. Sometimes we don't really want to know the answer, or we just don't want to wait.

As an immature believer, I skipped this step. I had attached myself in a financial way to a close family member without asking the Lord whether it was a good idea. After making several investments, I started feeling an inner urgency to separate myself and my investments from this relative. I wasn't sure this feeling was coming from the Lord because in the worldly sense everything seemed great.

I thought I knew best, but soon after ignoring the prompting, the situation took a sharp turn for the worse. I ended up more than $154,000 in debt.

I had made a huge mistake. It really *was* God trying to direct me through His Holy Spirit and I had not trusted Him. Though I quickly repented and asked God for forgiveness, the consequences remained. If I had only asked the Lord for help, listened to the Holy Spirit and obeyed, I would not have accumulated that excessive debt.

Whatever our excuses, the truth is God wants us to come to Him all the time. Jesus said, "I tell you, *keep on asking*, and you will receive what you ask for. *Keep on seeking*, and you will find. *Keep on knocking*, and the door will be opened to you. For everyone who asks, receives. Everyone who seeks, finds. And to everyone who knocks, the door will be opened," (Luke 11:9-10 NLT, emphasis mine).

Asking is the great effort He asks of us. If we invest time in seeking the Lord, He'll reward us for putting Him first.

Listening

The next step after asking is listening. "Anyone with ears to hear must listen to the Spirit and understand what he is saying," (Revelation 3:22 NLT).

To stay on God's path, we must keep close enough with Him to hear His directions. That means taking the time to develop a relationship. Isn't that the way we treat our spouses, families and friends? Which of them would appreciate seeing us for one hour on Sunday without any further communication the rest of the week? Having a relationship with a deep connection requires effort on our part. The more time we invest in it, the stronger the relationship will become.

Listening became a critical aspect in keeping my work life on track. Some time ago, I had a good job as a colonel in the US Air Force, directing over 1,200 military and civilian personnel in San Antonio, Texas. I had, however, reached the end of advancement within the organization. I still felt I had more to contribute, so I was excited when I learned of an available high-level civilian position in another organization—one that would be perfect for my skills and would result in a large promotion.

It seemed like an answer to prayer—a new position in line with my desire for advancement, along with more money to tithe into God's kingdom. I spent the entire week updating my resume and completing the intensive application to get it submitted by the end-of-the-week deadline.

The following Sunday, I went to church. The pastor's message, "The Mystery of the Open Door," challenged me to question whether I should automatically walk through a door just because it was open. I wondered if I'd been making assumptions about God's will for me and hurried home to pray.

As I sought the Lord, the Holy Spirit told me this job might seem acceptable, but it was not God's perfect path for me. While it seemed to satisfy my heart's desire for a promotion, it wasn't God's will that I take this opportunity. If I did, the distractions of the demanding position would serve to slow down my spiritual development and delay the fulfillment of the plan God had in mind.

That Monday, I removed my name from consideration.

Because I'd taken time to listen and wait, I was available to accept an amazing military leadership position in Afghanistan the Lord sent a short time later. This position allowed me to lead and serve others and gave me time to provide a great deal of ministry during my off hours. From there, the Lord quickly led me to retire as a colonel with thirty years of service with the US Air Force and enter full-time ministry.

Finding time every day to read God's Word and spending time in prayer is key to knowing Jesus and hearing His voice. Prayer is not just giving God a list of all the things we want Him to do for us. It also means spending some quiet time to listen and hear what He wants from us, as well.

Some people find it easiest to listen during their daily quiet time of prayer. Others hear God's voice better while listening to praise music or even prayer-walking outdoors. Personally, I journal—letting the Holy Spirit speak through my thoughts as I write.

Try different things until you find the way you most clearly hear from the Holy Spirit. Listen to Him every day so you don't run the risk of stepping onto a path that will take you farther from God instead of nearer.

And you will hear Him. Remember, Jesus said, "I am the good shepherd; I know my own sheep, and they know me. . . My sheep listen to my voice; I know them, and they follow me. I give them eternal life, and they will never perish. No one can snatch them away from me," (John 10:14–28 NLT).

Obeying

One year, while participating in an amazing short-term mission trip in the Philippines, the host organization announced they would be going to Nepal the next year for the first time. My heart leapt! It had always been one of my dreams to serve in Nepal, and I ached to visit the people and serve God there.

An open door to Nepal seemed to stand before me, yet I felt a check in my spirit—an urge to say no. I delayed signing up or paying the deposit because each time I went to the Lord, I sensed He did not want me to go. The deadline was quickly approaching. Why wouldn't He want me to take this trip?

Even during my time of prayer and fasting to seek His will, I couldn't shake the feeling this was not my time to go. I did sense His assurance, however, that another opportunity awaited me to minister there in the future. It was a difficult decision, but I chose to listen and obey. Now was not the time for me to go to Nepal.

I soon found out why the Holy Spirit had restrained me. Right before I would have been scheduled to take off for Nepal, a last-minute work crisis cropped up. Had I ignored God's prompting and signed up anyway, I would have had to cancel. The result would have been the loss of my deposit money, the addition of travel cancellation fees and the team losing a critical member.

A couple of years later, as promised, the Lord opened the right door for me to walk through. My service in Nepal resulted in significant ministry impacts and connections. What a great reward for asking, listening and obeying God as I waited on His timing.

Kingdom Takeaway

When we ask, listen and obey, we walk in God's perfect path and plan for our lives. Whether He opens this door, closes that, or just asks us to wait, we can trust His plan is perfect. "'For I know the plans I have for you,' declares the Lord, 'plans to prosper you and not to harm you, plans to give you hope and a future. Then you will call on me and come and pray to me, and I will listen to you. You will seek me and find me when you seek me with all your heart. I will be found by you,' declares the Lord," (Jeremiah 29:11–14 NIV).

The Apostle Paul told us to never stop praying (1 Thessalonians 5:17). That's because the Holy Spirit wants to be our constant companion. As you continue to pray, let Him connect with you in an all-encompassing way—your thoughts, desires and activities. Allow the Holy Spirit to guide you through all your decisions in life.

Keep asking. Keep listening. Keep obeying the Holy Spirit's leadings. When you do that, you will be walking in the will of God for your life.

Battle Scars

By Sue Chamberlain

Yet in all these things we are more than conquerors through Him who loved us.

(Romans 8:37 NKJV)

I often say life is like a book. I'm eighty-two years old. Some would say I am at the end of my book, but I like where I am and where I am going. There are still interesting, exciting chapters left to explore.

At sixty-five, society calls us senior citizens, deems us eligible for Medicare, and prepares to retire us. This gets some of us thinking our influence in the world is over by then. Fortunately, there's no age limit with God. He never stops dropping kingdom truths into our hearts—truths that can impact others.

It All Happened One Day

At seventy-two, I was about to learn something new. I was teaching a group of adults ranging from age thirty-five to fifty. What started as a six-week class kept going until it was one year and counting. God was blessing. I was happy. They were happy. And we were all growing in His kingdom.

In October of 2011, I went to the doctor to get my flu shot. While I was there, I asked her to check a lump for me that seemed to be changing. I wasn't too concerned about it. I was a cancer survivor from age forty-five. It had been twenty-seven years since then, and that diagnosis had only required a lumpectomy and radiation.

But, within a week, my life accelerated from a mundane flu shot to a double mastectomy, one year of chemotherapy, and twenty-five radiation treatments. I had cancer in both breasts.

And Then War Broke Out

As my body went through the routine of tests and appointments with specialists, my spirit went to war.

I considered myself to be rooted and grounded and strong in prayer. Still, I found myself fighting against doubt, fear and grief. It wasn't something I could voice to my husband, but I began questioning my prayers.

Was I really *praying* or just saying words? Did I really *believe* all the lessons I taught, or had I just been telling stories? Was God *really* able to deliver us from our infirmities?

As I sat alone one night praying, I asked, "Lord, *do* I believe? *Do* I trust you? Or have I just been telling *others* to trust you?"

Waiting quietly for His answer, I quietly recited Mark 9:24. "Lord, I believe. Help my unbelief." The words were coming from my innermost being—not from my body or my soul, but from my spirit. My heart leapt. I did believe! I do believe! I am a believer!

Declaring Victory

The first people I wanted to tell were those in my Sunday School Class. They were my kids, my family. I loved them and knew they loved me. I didn't want them to hear it from anyone else.

It was a good decision. They became my number one support group. Even the guys got involved. I have a picture of the backs of bald or almost bald heads sitting with me on a pew in the church. I'd lost my hair within three weeks, and you couldn't be in the picture if you had hair. I love that picture!

There were more battles to fight, but my heart was prepared. At the onset of treatment, my oncologist gave me the option to choose which day of the week I preferred to have for feeling my best. I immediately said "Sunday, because I teach young adults and I don't want to stop."

Because she scheduled my chemo and radiation for Mondays, I always felt strongest in time for my classes. In fact, I never missed a single meeting in the fifty-two weeks of treatment. It came close some days, but God always provided the strength and anointing.

Battle Scars

About six weeks into the treatment, I stepped out of the shower and looked—really looked—into the mirror.

I usually avoided it, putting on my wig and dressing quickly so I wouldn't have time to look at my reflection. This day, I stopped and gazed at the creature looking back at me.

I had no hair, no eyebrows, no breasts and no fingernails (I lost all 10 fingernails and the nails on both big toes). "There is nothing feminine about me," I thought. I never bothered to take myself to the beauty shop. There was no hair to fix, no nails for a manicure or pedicure. I felt like a non-person. As my eyes filled with tears, I thought, "This cancer has ravaged my body."

I was in despair for the first time. Then I heard that familiar strong, voice of authority in my spirit. "*Yes*, the cancer has ravaged your body. But it has *not* touched your spirit!"

I thought it over and then said it out loud. "*Yes*, the cancer has ravaged my body, but it has *not* touched my spirit." I repeated it again and again. Within minutes, it took root in my spirit and became truth—kingdom truth. I could see the eyes in the mirror begin to shine with joy and understanding. *This body really is just a shell, and I am a spirit dwelling inside it.* It *will pass away, but* I *will not!* I started laughing in the face of the devil. God had just given me a Truth I could share with others.

And that's just what I have used to encourage people with over the past ten years.

Kingdom Takeaway

Jesus knew we would face trouble on this earth. It doesn't matter what generation or what culture we live in—there will be trouble. He is asking us to trust Him. "Let not your heart be troubled, you believe in God, believe also in me," (John 14:1 NKJV).

How do you guard your spirit from being troubled? Repeat key Scriptures until they strike root in your heart? Gather a group of prayer warriors around you? Declare your victory and fight on?

Whatever difficult situations you face, always remember, don't let it touch your Spirit!

From Tragedy to Triumph

By Lana Heightley

Then Rizpah daughter of Aiah, the mother of two of the men, spread burlap on a rock and stayed there the entire harvest season. She prevented the scavenger birds from tearing at their bodies during the day and stopped wild animals from eating them at night.

(2 Samuel 21:10 NLT)

From the outside looking in, she had it all—social position, beauty, intelligence, and she was "married" to a king. Although a concubine, Rizpah was considered a legal wife because she had been given as a physical token of an alliance made between the rulers of two neighboring kingdoms. She was also the mother of two of the king's sons, which gave her royal status.

This arrangement, however favored it was, nevertheless meant Rizpah's future depended solely on one man—King Saul of Israel. It also meant that as a concubine, she was subject to times of loneliness, endless waiting and wondering if or when the king would visit her again. The days and nights were often long. Occasionally, she was the object of others' abuses. Her life, in short, was one of vulnerability. Slavery rather than freedom. She must have often pondered her future, what might be in store for her.

Then the unimaginable happened. King Saul was killed in battle alongside his son Jonathan in a war with the Philistines. Thoughts swirled in her head. What was to happen to her? With the king gone, who would decide? If she were given away, where would she go? Who would get her? What about her sons?

The culture was known for the practice of eliminating the former royal generation when a new ruler took over the kingship. Fear and panic ensued. Would her sons be slaughtered? Would she be displaced from her royal status, left alone to fight a battle of loneliness and poverty?

When David replaced Saul as king, the Israelite kingdom was in the midst of national strife and war. Even in the palace, contention, disagreements and quarreling were taking place. Soon it became apparent that several men from the palace and military wanted her as a prize. She felt trapped and wondered who would be next in line for the throne. Saul had taken her as a concubine as spoils from a battle many years ago and dutifully and lovingly cared for and provided for her, but otherwise she was powerless. King David already had seven wives. What was she to him?

David chose to keep Rizpah, but not as a concubine. He provided care for her. Her story of tragedy and triumph is recorded in 2 Samuel chapter 21, but it is part of a larger story rooted in Israel's past.

Saul's Sins Revealed

Not long after Saul's death, Rizpah was brought to the forefront again, this time due to her dead husband's "sins." During a time of famine, King David learned that Saul, who had become prideful and self-willed in the later years of his reign, had broken an oath that Joshua had made to the Gibeonites hundreds of years before. In Saul's "zeal" to protect his kingdom, he and his sons were guilty of attempted extermination.

Even though the Gibeonites had deceived Joshua (see Joshua 9) into making a peace treaty not to destroy them as the Israelites claimed and cleansed the Promised Land, the treaty was made as an oath, sworn in the presence of the LORD, the God of Israel. Joshua had not first consulted the Lord but had acted on his own instincts. Nevertheless, he sealed the oath with the name of the Lord, making it a binding legal agreement. When their deception was revealed, the Gibeonites were made slaves to serve the tabernacle in perpetuity as woodcutters and water carriers for the altar of the Lord.

The story of Saul's attempted extermination of the Gibeonites appears in 2 Samuel 9, but his sin was not known to King David until Israel was in its third year of famine. It was taking its toll on the economy, the vegetation and everything that needed water for survival. When David inquired of the Lord, the Lord told him about the broken oath. David quicky summoned the Gibeonites.

He asked them, "What can I do for you? How can I make amends so that you will bless the Lord's people again?" (2 Samuel 21:3 NLT). In response, they ask for the death of Saul's remaining sons and grandsons.

David complied by agreeing to give them seven sons of Saul who were eligible to pay the vengeance price. Among the seven were the two sons of Rizpah. The Gibeonites hung the men on the mountainside and left their bodies in the gallows-tree, rotting on an open hillside for all to see.

Rizpah's Faithfulness to Her Children

Pause the story for a moment. Imagine the trauma, chaos and terror Rizpah went through, knowing her sons were to be sacrificed for Saul's sin. How unfair! Why did her innocent sons have to pay for the sins of their father? Could two wrongs make a right? She must have felt many emotions, including hate, betrayal and anger. Once again, she had few rights and was powerless to control her destiny. She was a victim as well. She could not stop the fate of her sons. But there was something she *could* do, and she determined to do it.

With an empty but courageous spirit, Rizpah went into action, displaying a dramatic illustration of a mother's love. Everyone present during the hanging left the mountain, but not her. No curse would take her boys. No! Her motherly love refused to permit her sons to be shamed further or their bodies desecrated. Not wanting what remained of her sons to be torn by scavenger birds during the day or eaten by jackals during the night, she spread burlap on a rock and stayed there with them—from mid-April to early October—the entire harvest season.

Pause again. Can't you just see her there as the bodies began to change, becoming blackened, decayed and withered? Can you imagine her suffering? What was her mindset? Can you see her pounding her fist on her breast and crying loudly and inconsolably?

Rizpah knew that one of God's laws had been broken, the law demanding that anyone hanging on a tree must be buried before sunset of the same day. As her vigil turned into weeks and even months, she must have wondered if this incident would turn into a scandal for David. Her fate could be in jeopardy once again.

But she was determined. At whatever the cost, Rizpah wanted justice and dignity for her children, who were born royalty and were innocent of their father's sin.

David's Actions to Bring Justice

Where was the rain, David wondered? The executions had not brought the expected blessing of rain. He then heard of Rizpah and what she had done. He, too, realized that one of God's laws had been broken, and he needed to gather the seven executed sons of Saul and give them a proper burial. At the same time, moved and touched by her loyalty and courage, David realized that he needed to retrieve the bones of both Saul and his son Jonathan that had been carried away in battle into the northern kingdom and give them a decent burial, as well. It was only then that the rain came.

Hope in Resurrection

Rizpah's story is one of the most heart-moving stories in the Bible. It is a compelling and touching example of a mother caring for her children even in death. Centuries later, British poet Alfred Lord Tennyson (1808-1892) penned a poem he titled "Rizpah." One portion of it reads as follows:

"Flesh of my flesh was gone, but bone of my bone was left—

I stole them all from the lawyers—and you, will you call it a theft?—

My baby, the bones that had suck'd me, the bones that had laughed and had cried—

Theirs? O no! they are mine—not theirs—they had moved in my side."[1]

Since the Biblical Rizpah would have known the Israeli belief in resurrection, she must have believed she would see her sons again. Until then, she wanted them to know she'd done all she could to love and take care of the flesh of her flesh—even in death. Her action brings to mind the mother of Jesus, who stayed at the foot of the cross as her son Jesus was crucified, and the women who came to the garden tomb to take care of Jesus' body after his crucifixion.

---

[1] Rizpah Poem by Alfred Lord Tennyson (internetpoem.com)

These women all saw tragedy turn to triumph. Rizpah saw her sons buried with dignity and honor. The mother of Jesus saw her son raised to life in dignity and triumph.

Modern Day Rizpah

My sister Mary was raised in a joyful, godly home. She was a God chaser, and in her teens, she was a head-turner. Such beauty, with her clear, blue eyes. She grew up with ideals of a dreamer. Her world was one of innocence and wonder. She was the baby in the family for over ten years. Spoiled? Yes, I guess. Mom and Dad clearly responded to her every request.

Mary met her husband at church. He was a very handsome soldier with a striking smile and twinkling eyes. It was love at first sight—for both. After a three-month dating period, a wedding followed. Mary was sixteen.

Nine months later, the babies started coming. A total of seven, one right after another. Coming along with the babies came the trials of parenting, financial woes, time management and other demands of life, all normal—until Mary's husband began to drink. He would arrive home from work late and inebriated. Drinking became a way of life for him, and by the time the children were in their teens, he was a serious alcoholic.

Mary then discovered she was carrying another child. The child died just before birth, which exacerbated her already fragile mental health. She had a nervous breakdown, and it was followed by her husband's job losses, quarrels and demands, including forbidding church attendance. He openly flaunted his infidelities with berating speech toward her. As the years went by, matters became worse. Eventually a divorce ensued, and the love of Mary's life ended up on skid row in Los Angeles, broken and delirious from his addictions.

Mary went to work to support the family. She took a night job. Within months, she discovered that six of her seven children were experimenting with drugs. Their father had managed to come back from skid row and introduce the children to them. Subsequently, all but one became addicts with little hope in sight.

Meanwhile, Mary renewed her church attendance and remained extremely faithful. She had always taken the children to church, even as adults, if they were living with her. At times, she was legalistic. Her commitment to tithing in particular was humorous to the family. She would not rob God of one penny of her income! But her prayer life for her children was like Rizpah. Fasting and prayer was a way of life. She was determined to love them regardless of the jewelry they stole from her and the money missing from her wallet or bank account. She continued to enlist prayer partners for her children's salvation.

Over the years, one son went to prison for stealing, one son died from alcoholism at thirty-seven, another became an alcoholic and could barely hold a job, one daughter died while taking a heroin hit, and another son died of serious heart problems brought on by drugs. No matter what the circumstances facing her, Mary never stopped loving her children and believing they would one day return to the Lord.

Salvation for the Household

Mary died, but not before she saw her family come to Christ. The son who went to prison has been sober and living for the Lord for the past twenty years. The son who died from alcoholism repented on the way to the hospital, asking Jesus to forgive him. A third son, also an alcoholic, was in a serious motorcycle accident. While lying in the middle of a busy road, he prayed for God to save him. God did, and that son came back to the Lord! The daughter who was an addict took a hit because of a family argument and died from it, but she asked God to forgive her in her last breath. The son who had the heart issue, even though he had episodes of schizophrenia induced by drugs, managed to live a redeemed life up to the time of his death. Even Mary's husband in his last days somehow made his way to her front yard. She found him lying in her flower bed. She took him to the hospital and faithfully stayed with him for three days, leading him through repentance before he died. The one daughter who was never in the grips of drugs is a strong Christian, and her children are strong believers, as well.

Yes, Mary faced pain, terror, fear, broken-heartedness, sleeplessness and loss, but she lived to see her prayers for her family answered. As with Rizpah, tragedy turned into triumph.

Kingdom Takeaway

Donald Davidson, American philosopher (1917-2003), has said of Rizpah's story, "Beauty is often to be found in the most unexpected places, and here we find the blackness of that pre-Christian night pierced by a pure white shaft of sacrifice and love."[2]

When Jesus came to earth centuries later, the kingdom principles he taught his followers to live by were often not new. He knew the ancient truths revealed in Old Testament stories and brought them before us again. In Romans 8:28, we are told that "God causes everything to work together for the good of those who love God and are called according to his purpose for them."

Ask yourself the following questions.

1. What trauma or experience have you endured to stand as a faithful, loving woman for your family?
2. What tools did you employ then or are you employing today?
3. Have you applied unceasing prayer, considered prayer partners and exercised your authority over the evil one and his activities in your family?
4. How do you see yourself as a modern day Rizpah?

---

[2] Herbert Lockyer, *All the Women of the Bible* (Grand Rapids, MI: Zondervan Publishing House, 1988).

Crooked Crowns and Little Kingdoms

By JoAnne Meckstroth

Every human has a seed of greatness buried in a gift needed by the world.

—Myles Munroe

Date night was always an unexpected adventure, especially when four-year-old Lucas and nine-year-old Jacob were my dates.

"Where do you want to go tonight, boys?"

"Burger King," they said in unison.

The fast-food restaurant was their favorite. I knew their wiggles, giggles and playful punches would pepper the meal. Although I loved these times, an hour spent with burgers and fries was usually *Grandma's* limit.

Jacob ran ahead while I scooped up a colorful cardboard king's crown off the counter and plopped it on Lucas' head.

"Lucas, you're a king," I declared.

"I'm a king?" he asked with a puzzled look and wrinkled brow.

"Yes, you're a king!"

On the way home, he kept checking his reflection in the rearview mirror, excited to share his royal attire with his parents. With a slight swagger and a puffed-up chest, he announced himself.

"Look at me. I'm a king!"

Mom and dad bowed low, and the family dog rolled over in submission. Lucas saw the first benefit of his new status.

Needing a royal robe to match his crown, he put on his dad's red plaid bathrobe. With his cardboard crown askew and oversized robe in a puddle at his feet, he ruled over his small world.

He wasn't satisfied simply bearing the title of king. He needed a place to rule and reign. In the living room, using the coffee table, upside down chairs, and overstuffed sofa cushions, he created a child-sized, makeshift mountain. His final touch was to cover it all with brightly colored blankets stripped from his bed. Still, it leaned precariously. Throwing aside all caution, he climbed to the top, straightened his crown, and raised his arms in victory.

"This is my kingdom," he announced with gusto. Soon his manmade kingdom came tumbling down as he attempted to rule and reign on the unstable patch of land.

Called to Be Kings

While God calls us all kings, the degree to which we walk in that place of authority is dependent on us. How willing are we to step onto our patch of land and display His glory through our spiritual gifts, our natural talents and anointing? Even when our robe is too big and our paper crown a bit crumpled, He comes alongside to smooth out the wrinkles and enlarge our capacity to govern and showcase His kingdom.

According to Jesus, we are part of a kingdom of kings, and He is our King of kings. Here's how He described it in one story: "Then the King will turn to those on his right and say, 'You have a special place in my Father's heart. Come and experience the full inheritance of the kingdom realm that has been destined for you from before the foundation of the world!" (Matthew 25:34 TPT)

I experienced this Scripture firsthand at the age of twenty-nine. Being recently filled with the Holy Spirit, I felt the weight of the Father's love and sensed a measure of His fullness come upon me. It didn't happen just one time, but through a continual outpouring of His presence. Gradually, He brought me into a new dimension of His supernatural kingdom. In this new place I received greater understanding of the purpose and function of the spiritual gifts found in 1Corinthians 12: 9-11, and how these gifts empower God's people to live supernaturally in their practical, everyday lives.

Like Lucas, I passionately looked for my place to rule and reign. "Surely," I thought, "I've found the Promised Land."

Knowing the Enemy

When God told Joshua the Promised Land was his, He gave him the same guarantee He'd given to Moses: every place he put his foot would belong to him. (Joshua 1:3) There was a problem, though. The land was occupied. In order to put his foot down he needed to move someone else's boot. By force, if required. I felt like my challenge, unfortunately, would be even more difficult than Joshua's. The boots on *my* patch of land weren't the enemies'—they were my family's. Or so I thought.

Just like my grandson's makeshift kingdom, I had built an imaginary world around me. If I had a perfect family—a perfect church— a perfect ministry—then I would find that perfect place in God's kingdom. But first, I had to convince them to be who I wanted them to be.

In a million subtle and not-so-subtle ways, I tried to force change. I offered unsolicited advice and attempted to navigate (some might say manipulate) their lives without permission. Of course, they pushed back on my ideal and my makeshift kingdom came tumbling down.

Standing in the midst of the rubble I'd made, I realized I had been the boot in the way. I was my own worst enemy.

Backing Up to Move Forward

Battle-weary and discouraged, I decided living by God's standards had become far too difficult. On a hot summer day while our family picnicked with a group of friends in the local park, I decided to lay aside my faith and return to my old ways. This would be easy. With a case of beer already on ice and the children safe on the playground, I walked back to have a drink with my friends.

On the way, I complained and reaffirmed my bad attitude. *I'm angry with my family. My marriage is in crisis. My siblings pushed me away because my faith seemed too radical. God, I'm angry with you for not helping me create my perfect world. I thought Jesus was supposed to make my life better—instead my world is falling apart. I'm finished.*

Then the oddest thing happened. A stranger stepped in front of me and asked, "Are you a Christian?" No introduction. No social niceties. Just the question.

"Yes. Who are you?" I snapped.

"I knew it!" she said, walking away with a giggle.

For a moment, I was outraged. This stranger (I think she was an angel) spoiled my plans! I was ready to throw a really big tantrum, get drunk and have a pity party. This woman (the angel) looked me in the eyes and confronted my faith. She was a voice from heaven standing between me, and my destructive, downhill spiral. Her question and my confession of faith broke the enemy's foothold. What I thought would be an easy choice had become impossible. Thankfully, the Lord loved me too much to let me go my own way. Tears of repentance streaked my make-up and removed every bit of my black mascara. I was not a pretty sight, but I sure felt good!

You see, I had become so busy trying to fit God into my makeshift kingdom, I had laid aside the most important thing—my relationship with the King. In that moment, I chose to make Him central in my affections and decisions.

Our relationship no longer hinged on what He could do for me. It grew from a tiny seed into an intimate exchange of thoughts and ideas. He quieted my restless soul, and I welcomed His abiding presence. I talked about my deepest longings and struggles, and He taught me how to filter my thoughts through His Biblical principles.

As our relationship has continued to grow so has our trust in one another. He has trusted me with more—more wisdom, more power, more authority, more gifts and more assignments. He has led me through rough places and has shone His great light when times have grown dark.

Kingdom Takeaway

Do you have freedom in your relationship with the Lord? To desire freedom is not enough. You have to go after it. Your identity is wrapped up in how you have handled your personal struggles and triumphs. Jesus said, "The kingdom of heaven has suffered violence and violent men take it by force." In other words, the kingdom belongs to those who are willing to break through the devil's strongholds.

God also has a place for you to rule and reign in His kingdom here on earth. No matter what detours you may have taken on life's journey, He longs to bring you back "in step" with Him. He may even send an angel to help you.

There are seeds of greatness buried inside of you—hidden treasures waiting to be discovered. Whatever your spiritual gifts and natural talents are, He'll empower you to share them. The world needs you.

He will place an invisible crown—one more durable than cardboard—on your head and wrap you in His kingdom authority and power.

Then you can give a confident "yes" to the big question: "Are you a Christian?"

A Time to Act

By Melanie Boudreau

When we know that His plans are to prosper us and give us hope and future,
we bow down at once to the blessing of pruning,
knowing that the change that will take place in us, will take us places.

—Joshua Stannard

Many believers active in local, regional or global ministries have had to regroup because of the impacts of the pandemic.

Several years ago, I spent hours over the course of several days in a prayer grotto seeking God's direction. I wanted to know more specifically how to serve Him with some unique desires He had entrusted to me. I believed He had strategically positioned me with passion, vision, resources and favor to do a great kingdom work.

Praying, I wrote down what I heard in a fifteen-page document that became the basis for a global humanitarian and gospel project to be facilitated under a local foundation. I was excited to commit the remainder of my life to this vision—for the relief of its beneficiaries and to the glory of God.

Approved, launched and only a year into an impactful, successful mission, much of the world shifted from in-person to teleconferencing. It felt as if I was left holding the bag of a ministry idea God Himself had initiated—an empty bag that could not be adapted to the newly-emerging global protocols.

Vacillating, not knowing what to do, I wondered how ministers were to process the loss of access to the foreign field.

Then I recalled how Jesus appeared alive many times over a forty-day period after He rose from the dead. He repeatedly spoke to His apostles about God's kingdom, instructed them to wait for the promise of Holy Spirit to come and then ascended (Acts 1:1–9).

Poof. Gone.

Now What?

I felt a similar poof/absence dynamic in this instance.

Transition. Loss. Revelation. And then *poof.* Where did He go? What's next? What am I supposed to do?

I began to ask myself how the disciples knew what to do next in their time of loss and transition. The first thing they did was the last thing He told them to do. They waited. But they did not wait idly. "They all met together and were constantly united in prayer," (Acts 1:14 NLT).

The first chapter of Acts goes on to describe what else the disciples did while they waited. They chose a new disciple to replace Judas. Why? Did Jesus say, "Hey, fellows, as soon as I am gone, I need you to run an ad. You are one disciple short,"?

No. They identified their situation with a story in Scripture. In union with God, abiding with Christ in prayer, they looked at passages in Psalms and read about Judas' betrayal. "Let someone else take his position," (Psalm 109:8 NLT). Then they acted.

How About Us?

What if we could find our era prophetically described in Scripture, too? I am waiting to see how the dust settles to determine how to carry on with some version of the original ministerial vision God gave me (because I believe I heard God the first time). But I am not just waiting. I am praying, fasting and seeking God for the next, perhaps even bolder steps to take—steps which may require more faith than ever before. I am also prayerfully considering the description of the latter days in His written Word and acting on what I believe is happening next. In the process, He is taking me places I did not expect to go, even without international travel.

Kingdom Takeaway

We are all in a time of loss and transition to one degree or another. Your foundations may have been shaken this year. You may be trying to reorient yourself so you can follow after Christ more closely. He is, after all, your only true, secure foundation. You may be waiting on revival or on a powerful manifestation of His Spirit poured out for a great end-time harvest.

After losing Judas, the disciples discovered what to do next through the Word of God. They saw their place in Scriptural history and took action. We are to do the same—recognize our time in history Scripturally and take action according to what God says the Church is doing now. Like the disciples, you are not positioned to merely wait, but to pray and listen then take action as you align with the Word of God.

Will you explore where we are on the timeline of Scripture as you abide in Christ, then activate what He says believers are doing in our day?

What's On Your Bucket List?

By Frances Hallgren

I have come to give you everything in abundance, more than you expect—
life in its fullness until you overflow!

(John 10:10 TPT)

Most of us have heard about bucket lists. More than a few movies have been made about various people (even young folks) checking things off their lists. I got to thinking one day, "I don't have a bucket list. Do I need one? What would I put on it, anyway?"

Well, I looked around to see what other people put on theirs. Though certainly not an exhaustive list, here are a few of the things I found folks recording:

- Sky dive.
- Fly in a hot air balloon.
- Lose weight.
- Write a book.
- Fix a relationship.
- Have an OBE (out of body experience). Yikes!

Hmmm. It's like planning your highlights for a lifetime. People don't want to get to the end of their lives feeling their days had passed them by without something tangible or experiential to speak of.

Apparently, it's a way to assure we live life to the fullest and a reminder of all the things we want to achieve in our limited time on earth. Instead of wasting our time with pointless activities, we direct them fully toward what matters most to us.

That's a good thing. Right? Like, what if you were to die tomorrow? You wouldn't want untidy endings and end-of-life regrets.

My sister Susie's husband, Harold, died suddenly and unexpectedly. As she was going through his things, she came across a pocket Bible—one he had gotten as a soldier in the Army. Inside the cover she read some penciled notes, one of which was, "Visit Alaska." He never fulfilled his desire in life.

So, when Susie visited me at my home in Alaska a few months after his death, she brought some of his ashes with her. Together we sprinkled them in a peaceful, serene place we found alongside the Clearwater River.

It was a beautiful thing to do, and I was glad to be there to support my sister in this time of grief. Forgive me, though. I'll bet he would have enjoyed this visit much more when he was alive. And my sister, Susie, would have, too.

Is That All There Is?

I've never really been a fan of bucket lists. Somehow, the idea just made me hear Peggy Lee singing, "Is That All There Is?" in the back of my mind.

But that is *not* all there is for those living life in Christ. We have so much more than a mundane life on this planet. Jesus said, "I have come to give you everything in abundance, more than you expect, life in its fullness until you overflow!" (John 10:10 TPT) That alone makes me want to exchange my plans for the ones He has for me.

He also said, "If you, imperfect as you are, know how to lovingly take care of your children and give them what's best, how much more ready is your heavenly Father to give wonderful gifts to those who ask him?" (Matthew 7:11 TPT) The Apostle James echoes the idea. "Every gift God freely gives us is good and perfect, streaming down from the Father of lights," (James 1:17 TPT).

Bottom line? You can trust Him with your hopes, your dreams, your relationships, your life!

A New Kind of Bucket List

Until I looked into it more, I was happy to tell everyone that I didn't have a bucket list. After all, God had *so* surpassed anything I could have thought of, why limit Him with lists? I just left it all up to Him.

Now, however, I see there *is* value in making such a list—*if* I let the Holy Spirit guide me in making it. He causes me to consider deeper, more fulfilling and even eternal things to put on my list, so I can let go of carnal and superfluous ideas. He helps me focus on what is not only important, but really delightful. Meanwhile, He makes sure to insert joy and fulfillment in the mundane things in my life.

Kingdom Takeaway

Why don't you try it? Think for a moment. If you had unlimited time and resources, what would you put on your bucket list? (Remember, your Father in heaven actually *is* unlimited!) Ask the Holy Spirit to guide you as you dream. What *could* you put on that list? Spend a few minutes with the Holy Spirit. What would you do, what might you learn, what would you fix or experience for yourself? What fills your life with greatest meaning or joy? Write it all down.

Everything on your Holy Spirit-inspired list is achievable!

Of course, the most important thing to do before kicking the bucket is to have the assurance of heaven after you die. If you have invited Jesus Christ into your heart and made Him the Lord of your life, there will be no end-of-life regrets.

That said, we also can have abundant life here and now. When you give your plans, hopes, dreams, desires, wishes and prayers to Him, He will direct your steps. Proverbs 3:5 says, "Trust in the Lord completely, and do not rely on your own opinions. With all your heart rely on him to guide you, and he will lead you in every decision you make," (TPT).

You will be totally amazed at what He will do!

"No eye has ever seen, and no ear has ever heard, and it has never occurred to the human heart all the things God prepared for those who love Him," (1 Corinthians 2:9, the Voice).

Mind-blowing stuff, people!

Adversity: A Springboard to Success

By Sarah Williams

But that's not all! Even in times of trouble we have a joyful confidence, knowing that our pressures will develop in us patient endurance. And patient endurance will refine our character, and proven character leads us back to hope. And this hope is not a disappointing fantasy, because we can now experience the endless love of God cascading into our hearts through the Holy Spirit who lives in us!

(Romans 5:3–5 TPT)

"You have cancer." Three words no one ever wants to hear.

"What?" I shook my head. "Could you check the name on that chart again?" This can't be possible. I hadn't detected any lumps, had no history of breast cancer in my family and I felt just fine.

It was hard to believe these words had just been spoken to me—Sarah. After a flurry of additional tests, doctor visits and biopsies, the dreaded diagnosis was confirmed. It was worse than expected.

"Sarah, because you have multiple sites of cancer, we will have to do a double mastectomy."

Fear socked me in the stomach like a clenched fist. Frantic thoughts swirled around in my head creating a thundering pressure between my ears. A dark tornado threatened to tear apart the wonderful life Barry and I had built. How do I navigate through this frightening news? Who do I tell and how do I tell them, "Oh, by the way, I have breast cancer"?

What about Barry? He's not only my husband and Mr. Wonderful—he's my business partner. I can't be sick. He needs me. The business needs me.

Well-meaning platitudes did nothing to calm my spirit. I needed the raw power of God to muffle my fears.

A few weeks later, while leading a local gathering to pray for our nation, I experienced that kind of fresh power. At the end of the meeting, three men came up and prayed for me. It was a supernatural moment. I literally felt the invasive fear and anxiety leave me and the supernatural faith and peace of the Holy Spirit take its place.

It was a miracle, and I can honestly say, I was never afraid again. The nurses were amazed that my blood pressure remained normal, even as I headed into surgery.

A Divine Connection

One of my hardest choices was determining what kind of surgery to have. Swamped with information, drowning in options, I felt trapped in indecision. Do I get a double mastectomy? Do I have implants? Do I have DIEP flap surgery where part of your stomach area becomes your new breasts? (Amazing, right?)

What was the best choice, and how could I decide?

Still weighing the pros and cons of each option, I visited the store that provides prosthetics for mastectomy patients. As I explained my indecision to the store clerk, a young woman about thirty-five years old interrupted my conversation.

"I'm sorry. I overheard what you were saying, and I just wanted to tell you how sorry I am! I had a double mastectomy six months ago."

She drew me into her arms, and together we cried over the unexpected loss of our breasts. This was my only meltdown. We shed tears over the huge interruptions in our lives. We cried over the uncertainty and the pain of surgery and chemotherapy. She was a woman who knew exactly what I was going through! She understood every emotion I had and had struggled over the same indecisions I was now facing.

"Do you want to see my scar?"

I nodded.

In the dressing room, she pulled up her blouse and showed me the aftereffects of her surgery. I braced myself for the worst. Scars can impact a woman's psychological and emotional recovery, but I found myself both surprised and comforted. She bore a simple scar across her chest. Not nearly as horrific as I thought it might be.

"Okay! I can do this!"

My choice was clear. No more surgery. I'd deal with the scars.

A Different Kind of Tears

I have cried many times since that day in the store. However, my tears haven't been over my loss, but rather over the goodness of God, who showed how much He loved me. Just think about it—He brought that woman from Pendleton, Oregon to Spokane, Washington (three hours away) at the exact time I needed her. She had intended to be in the store the day before, but because the store was closed when she got there, she had to return the next day.

This young woman was God's gift to me. As I continue on my healing journey, she has been a source of support. She's called, sent cards and even mailed me a chemo survival package. I am truly grateful for this God-found friendship.

Only Gratitude

Six weeks after my surgery, I thought my journey was nearing completion. But in a follow-up visit, I was told I'd need chemo. This meant I would lose every strand of my thick, blonde hair. I'd struggle with exhaustion, a racing heartbeat, and a myriad of other side effects, some of which continue today. Plus, I've had to get fitted for the right kind of wig and stare at my balding head and flat chest every night.

But today, I am so very thankful.

I'm thankful for my strong, caring husband who tended to my every need. He was my nurse, my housekeeper, my cook and prayer warrior. He kept relatives and friends informed, prayed over me and worked when I couldn't. He was at every doctor appointment and chemo treatment. But most importantly, he loved me. He kissed me every morning and every night.

"Sarah, I love you! We will get through this together."

I'm thankful for amazing, caring, doctors and nurses. I felt their compassion and was strengthened by their knowledge and encouragement.

I'm thankful for God's timing. I love being with people, and since my healing process took place during the Covid 19 lockdown, I didn't feel so isolated. Everyone else was in a similar situation, since most people weren't out and about anyway.

Most of all, I'm thankful to my Lord and Savior because I know I am in His hands, now and forever.

Through it all, my faith is stronger and deeper, and I have a clearer sense of the limited time we have on earth. I want to have more intimate conversations with others and with my Jesus. I want to share more with the younger generations and teach them what I have learned so they might go farther and higher. I want to have more impact for the kingdom of God.

Adversity: A Seedbed of Opportunity

There is a term called *The Adversity Effect.* It defines adversity as the seedbed of opportunity. To say it another way, bad circumstances will change us, but how it changes us depends on our personal perspective.

Mark Batterson, in his book *In a Pit with a Lion on a Snowy Day*, wrote about Alfred Alder. Alder was a researcher and scientist who believed birth defects, poverty, illnesses and negative circumstances often prove to be the springboard of success. At the turn of the 20th century, he did a study on optical anomalies. During his research, he discovered that seventy percent of the art students he studied had suffered from this abnormality. He also found degenerative traces in the ears of great composers like Mozart and Beethoven. Then he cited numerous examples of other people who eventually became successful in the area of their greatest weaknesses.

How about you? Have you in the past, or are you contending right now with, negative circumstances?

How do you handle adversity? Do you rise up and fight? I've been through such deep hurt I thought my heart would break. I have been through financial distress where I woke up every night in a cold sweat for fear we couldn't pay our bills. Some of the most difficult hardships have come from the religious community, where I have been misunderstood, wrongly accused and shamed by religious leaders and a congregation.

How do we learn and grow in the midst of trouble? First, I believe God wants to encourage us and will send us a miracle if we look for it.

I have a friend who went through cancer treatment. She told me about a stranger who came up to her in the grocery store and told her, "God knows this is a difficult time and He wants you to know He has your back!"

Another friend has a love of ladybugs, and in the midst of what she was going though, ladybugs showed up in the most unexpected places. God knows how to speak to the heart of each of us in order to reassure us. And I have learned: He will speak.

Secondly, there may be days when it seems impossible to pray. It's all you can do to just put one foot in front of the other. That's okay! God knows our weaknesses. He is so gracious and is always interceding for us. Even though you may not be able to sense it, His presence doesn't leave you. There are times when, "having done all, stand firm."

Third, play good worship music and speak in tongues. You may even just cry your way through this, but your focus returns to the goodness and the power of God. And though fear will try to overwhelm you, think about those things that are true, honorable, good and admirable. Speak out those verses you have learned through the years. Rehearse your testimonies of His intervention in your life in the past. Strength and faith will return.

Fourth, know you will go through the valley and come out on the other side. In these times, I believe God is deepening our roots in Him, increasing our trust in Him and working in our heart to be more like Him.

These difficult circumstances have changed me. I am more aware God not only sees me, but He cares for and loves me unconditionally. I am more confident because He has clothed me with His ability, His power and His heavenly success. Most of all, He has made me more compassionate and much less judgmental.

Kingdom Takeaway

Remember, your most difficult challenges can set you up for your greatest successes, especially when you see your circumstances from God's perspective. They will teach and reposition you for a greater God thing—where impossibilities move into the possible realm and miracles occur. There, beauty and order hover over chaos, waiting to land and fill the void.

You are a byproduct of the way you think of God. Is He limitless? Always loving? Always faithful? Do you feel He really cares about you? Your picture of God will determine who you can become. As you face challenges and see the hand of God, He becomes bigger.

Adversities are actually opportunities for God to reveal Himself in greater measure. He planned for every contingency you may ever encounter. While we have no idea what is coming next, take comfort that God knows. It's all planned out.

Even though it may not make sense, God is more interested in getting you to a specific place and in your maturity in Him than you are. He wants to take those difficult circumstances and set you up for success. His eyes are on you. He is ordering your footsteps. He has a destiny for you.

What are you focusing on? Can you put your eyes on Him instead of your circumstances? Can you choose to trust His endless love? Can you believe that God will bring you through your circumstances? And that you are being purified in the fire?

It's been over a year now, and still, I've not feared. Faith has anchored me within the invisible realm and has brought me into agreement with the mind of God.

I can say with all confidence "cancer will not—*cannot* intimidate me."

Running with Horses

By Pam Eichorn

If you are worn out after only running with a few men,
how will you one day compete against horses?
If you stumble on the easy terrain,
how will you manage in the thick brush near the Jordan?

(Jeremiah 12:5 The Voice)

Have you ever seen the movie *Ben Hur*? There are scenes with chariot horses that have much to teach us about leadership.

One of these is when Judah Ben Hur first catches a glimpse of four beautiful white horses training in the desert. Hitched side-by-side, they pound through the straightaway but cannot complete the turn.

Judah tells the horses' owner they're in the wrong positions. Instead of maximizing their combined strengths, they are working against one another.

Later, the horses prance into their master's tent to say goodnight. As the Arab caresses each one, he brags on them to his guest. This one is the slowest but can run all day without tiring. The next is the swiftest. That one is happy-go-lucky and the last one is as steady as they come.

Judah is finally put in charge of their training. He rearranges how they're harnessed, taking each one's strengths into account. They must, he reminds them, be prepared to go around the track in Rome nine times.

Setting the slowest in place as the team's anchor, Judah tells the stallion he is their rock—steady and strong. Then he reminds the swiftest that he isn't running alone. His place among the others isn't to get them across the finish line their first time around the track but the last. As he harnesses the happy-go-lucky horse, Judah praises him for not letting anything interfere with his zeal to just to do his work and enjoy it. Finally, he lines up the last horse, where his steadfastness will pull on the others to keep them all going.

When they finally enter the arena in Rome, the team is harnessed and aligned. Together, they roar to success in one of the last scenes. All the pieces—man, horses, and chariot—are finally working together, fighting the battle to win the race.

The Chariot Team of the Church

I can't help but think how true this sometimes is about the church. We do well on the straightaways when everyone runs their best. But if we are out of position, we won't make the turn needed for the final stretch.

How exciting will it be to know you are exactly where you should be? What an encouragement to look to your left and right to those fighting beside you. In many dystopian movies like *Lord of the Rings* or *Narnia*, this powerful truth is at play. The kings, the leaders of the day, don't stay on a hill watching. They fight in the battle, swinging swords and dying next to those they lead.

Many ministries begin with everyone working together, learning together and building together. They work as one, operating in a type of synergy that propels everyone forward. We'd do well to remember these beginnings and not let anything move us into positions for which we're ill-suited. This way, we'll always be in a place where we can function as one.

David's mighty men fought like this. Though they fought separately, they battled in the kingdom for the kingdom, forming a unity we seldom see in today's world. Operating as a single entity, they were true to who they were but also true to David and the kingdom.

Kingdom Takeaway

Most of David's mighty men (listed in 2 Samuel 23:8–38) began as misfits. They grew to adore David because he not only cared for, defended and fought for them, but because he knew how to follow his own leader—God. The horses in *Ben Hur* responded similarly to their leader. They loved him because he treated them well, recognized their abilities and understood how to position them so they could run their best.

As leaders, our job is to equip each one under us to be their best—not just for their individual battles lying ahead but also for corporate ones. Greatness is often inspired by the quality and integrity of leadership. How do you inspire those you are leading? Do they see you adjust your position at times to produce the best outcome?

Have you seen teams who are effective at working together—who draw one another to their best? Can you identify a common denominator? I'm guessing these team members not only respect their leaders but feel safe with them.

How are you as a leader at making others feel safe? Are you willing to change and improve to be a better leader? If you are, others will come to you because of what you can help them become.

Dutch's Sheets, in his daily program *Give Him 15*, said this: "It's time for us to *be* what we've been becoming. Take your place, step into the wind and watch God launch you into the destiny He has been seeing for you all along."

Think about watching the clips of *Ben Hur* I wrote about for inspiration. (If you are really brave, watch the final race. It gets a bit bloody, but all battles do.)

Then saddle up, find your position, and ride!

Lovin' My Loud

By Valerie Johnson

"Only a man with nothing to hide could make that kind of racket."

—Sara Sheridan

I was in my twenties when my hairdresser witnessed the love and forgiveness of God through the cross of Jesus Christ to me. Oh, happy days!

As a newborn babe in Christ, I had zeal, zeal and more zeal. I loved to pray and dance before the Lord (King David didn't have anything over me). I'd sing praises and tell my testimony to anyone who would listen. You know, the word testimony means *do it again*, and that's what I do—again and again, I tell my story and share my love for Him.

Expressing My Loud

I love going to all types of gatherings where the gifts of the spirit are in full bloom. I want to be anywhere the power of God is in action—whether it's hearing the Word, prayer meetings, miracle healing encounters or a deliverance service.

Now friends, I'm a black woman, and when God's in the house, there's no way I can hide my excitement. I pray, you know, *loud*. Read the word of God *loud*. Rebuke the devil, even *louder*! I even fast loud! I don't know why I am so loud. Maybe I think God doesn't hear me or He's just too busy to hear me when things are too quiet.

The Backstory

I just told you the "now" part of my story. But let me take you back to my childhood and early adult life.

When that hairdresser told me about the redemption power of Jesus, it was not the first time I'd heard that message. Looking back at my early years, I was practically immersed in the "God lifestyle." My sister was known as "that holy roller." She would pray out loud all the time and take her dancing shoes to church.

Some days it seemed as if she'd stay there from sunrise to sunset. When that wasn't long enough, there would always be a midnight prayer watch for her to attend. My mom, on the other hand, was a powerful prophet. When she'd prophesy in church, everyone stood up inside. She'd foretell many events that came to pass. Do you believe it?! Someone actually started selling tickets to get in a line to get a word from her! When she found out, it hurt her deeply and she backed away from the congregation, but she continued to love and serve God. Every morning I'd see her at her altar—our kitchen table—praying and seeking God with her Bible in hand. Yep. They were both full of passion…and loud.

In my younger days, I attended a traditional Christian church on the corner of my neighborhood block. It was *NOT* one of those radical Pentecostal churches my sister and mom had attended. My people seemed kinder and more reverent, in my way of thinking.

In spite of my resistance and lack of enthusiasm, my "holy roller" sister was always dragging me off to some hot, high-praise type meeting. You'd think that would have trained me up in the way I should go, but no. None of this had any impact on me. I was religious, you see. I ran back to my neighborhood church. It felt like it would be a safe place where no one would challenge me to take risks for God. And no one would judge me when I chose to just show up, even if it was just on occasion.

Although I had these two powerful women in my life, what I really heard them say was that I was a sinner and needed to repent. As a result, I thought God could only love me if I did everything right, or at the least stopped doing everything wrong. I thought I'd never be good enough. Whenever something bad would happen, I thought God was showing His disapproval of me.

This way of thinking was reinforced when my older sister (That's right, the loud, holy roller one) got pregnant out of wedlock. I saw another side of those two women. Mom continually threw up my sister's sin in her face. Something clearly wasn't working about this God thing. Here were two women, saved and loving God, leaders in the church, and both acting unkind and unloving to one another. I thought I was crazy to trust God.

God's unconditional love had never been explained to me, nor had it been acted out when things got tough in my home. So why try? I decided I wanted nothing more to do with church. Until…that amazing day I said yes to Jesus.

Pray until God Shows Up

In spite of a few bumps in the road, while growing up with these two passionate women—Mom and my older sister—I learned a very important principle—When you pray, expect God to show up and do something! As would be expected, like them, I too became a bold woman of prayer. Loud, of course!

As ambassadors of heaven, we are commissioned by the Father to live like the kingdom of heaven has come to earth. This happens when we lean into the Holy Spirit in prayer, in an intentional pursuit to fulfill kingdom business. As Charles Spurgeon said, even Christ waited to preach until he had spent nights in intercessory prayer and uttered strong (that means loud) cries and tears for the salvation of his hearers. Regardless of how we feel or how big the sacrifice may be, He moves us forward to live for His kingdom.

The Bible says that men ought always to pray, but sometimes we do so out of obligation. The alarm clock sounds, and we fall on our knees like robots. I am convinced, through over thirty years of faith, prayer is a lot more than what we have experienced so far.

There is no doubt prayer is a powerful weapon that can be easily misused. Using it properly will help align things on earth with the kingdom. It's more than praying or fasting once and expecting Daddy God to pour out the things on our wish lists. Prayer turns our impossibilities into God's possibilities.

For me, prayer calls me into focus. It clarifies the intentions of my mind, will and emotions, and engages the Holy Spirit to come and advocate for me. He pleads my case and prays through me.

Some of you may still be trying to get God's attention. That used to be my attitude. The louder I prayed, the better I thought He might hear me. Except *loud* didn't seem to make any difference. My prayers weren't answered any faster than the sweet, quiet petitions of my prayer partners. I began to wonder how my loud ways would turn into my dream about going to the nations?

More than anything, I wanted to be used by God, but that kind of loud behavior might be a distraction. *Right, God? Okay*, I thought. *No more being loud*! It had to stop.

Prevailing Prayer

I travailed and prevailed. But the more I asked God to fix me, the louder I got. My pity parties were not only loud—they were pathetic. I wanted to be quiet and pretty when I prayed. I didn't want soggy beads of sweat running down my hairline and dripping off my chin. But it just seemed to happen. Maybe something else was wrong. After all, only about thirty percent of my loud prayers were being answered—and that thirty percent was about things I barely prayed about!

My childhood lessons haunted me. *I don't have enough faith. I'm not privileged enough. I haven't given enough money in tithes and offerings.* These had to be the reasons I wasn't receiving answers.

During one of many complaint sessions, the Holy Spirit said, "Stop it with all your unbelief! Stop it! Let Me guide and teach you how to go inside of Me in prayer, instead of looking from the outside and never involving Me."

What? I thought I was praying the way I should.

Okay, I'm really tired Lord. You are going to have to teach me how to break through this thing called prevailing prayer.

An, by the way, I'm tired of praying and praying and not seeing enough happen!

Consecration

I decided to set aside a "dedicated time" to fast and pray. I knew it wasn't going to be easy. I had never been able to stay focused for long periods on anything. I felt different from others when it came to fasting and prayer. Why did the dedication of time to the Lord have to be so hard for me? Whenever I tried turning off the world and going deeper with God, I'd start thinking of all the things I'd done wrong. I couldn't shake my doubts and would have flashbacks of what hadn't worked in the past. Or I worried. I worried about things that hadn't happened or even things I was afraid *would* happen.

Time to battle!

My vacation days were approved, and my calendar was cleared of appointments. Armed with spring water, lemons, molasses, my favorite Bible and new journals to write in, I was ready!

The first day, nothing happened. I couldn't pray because I was too hungry. I thought about food all day long. The second day, I fasted until 6:00 in the evening. On the third day, I prayed all day until 7:00 in the evening and then ate a meal. Finally, I managed to go a whole day without food. *At last!* I thought, *I'm "queen of the breakthrough!"* I'd love to say the rest of the time I flew into heaven and sat at the feet of Jesus. But that isn't what happened. I did, however, find out a few things God wanted from me.

What God Wanted

He wanted me to understand that getting His attention is not about a fast. It's not about how long I pray, how loud I pray or how much I sweat. It's all about knowing Him, trusting Him and learning to love myself as He so loves me. It's about letting loose the bands of the "me" who sabotages myself—the "me" who prevents my heart from knowing I am worthy to be loved, blessed and used by Him. The battle wasn't over. I realized false thoughts from the accuser had hindered my faith, and my mind needed regeneration. My thoughts needed to stay on Him.

Change Happens

Days later, I still sensed His Spirit lingering and felt closer to God than at any other time in my life. I sensed the heart of God and the mind of God, but when had the change occurred? While I'd been looking for bells and whistles—something spectacularly supernatural—all the while, transformation was taking place in the quietness of the Holy Spirit. And yes, it was happening in the loudness of my personality as I cried out for more! All I was seeking after appeared in my refusal to give up—in my saying, "Lord, thank you for making me wonderful in your eyes. Thank you."

Wasted Days and Wasted Nights

How much time had I spent wanting to be something other than what God made me to be? All those years, I'd failed to realize I was already walking in power with Him. I had failed to appreciate how lovely and beautiful He had made me. Loud. Bold. Passionate.

The enemy had tried to bind me to an image that was not who God had created me to be. But when I went to Daddy God, He showed me who He was inside of me. I'm convinced He's not in the least bit offended by my loudness. He'll never turn away because I'm not good enough. I always have His attention. He loves me loud and proud, yesterday, today and forever.

Kingdom Takeaway

Have you held back because you felt you weren't good enough for God? You may have a few quirky traits, and the devil has deceived you into thinking you aren't useable. I'm here to tell you it's a big fat lie. God will use your unique ways for His glory. You are His ambassador, and He has equipped you to bring the kingdom of God to earth.

So today, my friend, will you align your heart and mind on His kingdom purposes? With the Holy Spirit as our partner, let's lean in and connect with His heart for the people and nations of the earth. Let's discover what He wants to accomplish through us. Seek Him, alert to what He wants you to do to advance His kingdom on earth. Whether you are soft and sweet or loud and sweaty, God will empower you to fulfill His mandate.

Pray with me.

Dear Lord, I'm asking you to help me to keep my mind renewed with your holy Word and promises. I trust you. I know you love me just the way I am. Help me identify with that good thing you created in me and for me. Holy Spirit, thank you for your guidance and the gift of your comfort as I pursue my call and kingdom purpose. In Yeshua's name. Amen.

Set your hearts on things above, where Christ is seated at the right hand of God. Set your minds on things above, not on earthly things. (Colossians 3:1–2 NIV)

Coming Home: The Journey of a Prodigal

By Rosemarie Waters

Jesus said "I am the Way, the Truth and the Life.
No one may come to the Father except through me."

(John 14:6 NIV)

"The Universe Provides." The cloud-adorned sweater hung from the rack at a local store. Three years ago, I would have purchased that sweater and worn it with pride, but seeing this statement now made my heart sink. The New Age spiritual movement has used seemingly harmless platitudes like these to grip the souls of tens of thousands.

I know. I used to be one of them.

Oh, how the adult me wishes I had taken John 14:6 to heart back in my church's youth group days. The path I chose instead led me on a downward slope through a deep, dark valley. In the end, it was by God's grace that I stepped into the light-filled place for which my spirit had always been searching.

Here is my story.

New Age Attractions

New Age's focus on internal energy and a higher (but unknown) power proved a powerful draw for my curiosity. Elements of Eastern religions, with their peaceful pacifism and calming bells, blended with ideas such as reincarnation, the rejection of hell, and karma (works without salvation). I thought, "What harm could it do to try this?"

The spiritual lifestyle fascinated me. It was filled with tarot cards, yoga, meditation, reiki energy healing and mind-expanding drugs and alcohol. I carried polished stones in my pockets, rubbing them to call on the energy and power I believed they held. Rose quartz was supposed to represent love and could transform negative emotions into positive ones. The Tiger's eye was a beautiful stone supposedly holding self-confidence and inner strength.

I used various stones in my meditation practices or just carried them to intensify my sense of wellbeing.

Boy, the enemy sure knew how to hook me. New Age ideas drew me in through energy forecasts, meditation, yoga and crystals. The more I read and shared my spiritual experiences, the more my inner circle expanded with likeminded people. I was addicted to the promise of inner peace and guidance. Like a sponge, I soaked the toxic waters of demonic influence deep into my fibers.

Influence Deepens

While visiting friends in Colorado in 2015, I had my first tarot card reading. As I talked about my weight issues, the reader flipped card after card, telling me the numbers and imagery on each one. He finished by telling me how he'd read a book and lost twenty pounds. The idea of solving my weight problems so easily hung before me like a shimmering lure. I was also at my wit's end with allergies. When I found a book explaining how to read my body's symptoms and heal it with food, I lost sixty pounds in a year. *Really*!

The book wasn't New Age, but it completely changed my lifestyle and eating habits. It reinforced my belief that reading and seeking were spiritual routes to a "higher" path for me.

The hook was set, and I began collaborating with a friend who was a massage therapist like me. Something about this friend drew me deeper into these practices. Over time, our bond grew as we traded massages and shared healthy lifestyle topics. Together, we daydreamed about the "perfect business" and opened our medical massage operation in 2017.

The universe was clearly blessing me! I attributed my success to names like "the source" and "the divine."

My plunge into the spiritual realm continued and I eventually paid for another psychic reading. The psychic's words empowered me as she related my identity to various spirit animals. An eagle, because I had a higher perspective. The cat totem, because it represented elegance, curiosity, independence, protection, magic and other notable qualities. I resonated with the characteristics of every animal she called forward.

She went on to speak in detail about the injuries I'd dealt with for years—left SI pain, left knee pain. "Wow!" I thought. "She's the real deal!"

With my identity firmly connected to something I could learn more about, I was excited to build on my image of self-understanding. Little did I know, demonic sources were tickling my ears with just enough "truth" to keep me hooked. Satan dangled what I thought was my heart's desire before my eyes. He wanted my identity linked to the attributes of cats and birds rather than to giftings and talents from God. He convinced me I could get, through positive thoughts and the aid of stones and picture cards, what God had already given through creation and salvation through Jesus.

My comfort came from rubbing stones instead of from the Holy Spirit. I was making deals with the devil, not trusting in God and His perfect timing. Fortunately, God was about to show me a fork in the road I was traveling. Instead of heading into deeper shadows, this path would take me uphill to a brightness in the distance.

A Way Out

March 15, 2019, marked my turning point. I was visiting a longtime friend when she asked what I thought was an easy question. "What do you believe?"

I gave her my well-practiced answer. "Oh, I believe I am love-centered, that everything I do comes from the intention of love." When she asked what I thought of yoga as a spiritual practice, I said, "I do yoga because of the health benefits for my body. I don't see it as spiritual."

Then she told me about a yoga instructor that was well-known in the healthy lifestyle world. The deeper this woman had gone into practicing meditation and yoga the more demonic experiences she had. When she gave her life to Jesus, He set her free from that oppression.

Jesus. That was a name I hadn't considered since I was fourteen years old. My family church had been in turmoil in those days. When the youth pastor left the church, so did I. I was like the prodigal son in Luke 15. I wanted to do life my way. Not the church's way. Not my mom's way.

Instead of going after Jesus, I had pursued alcohol and drugs and dating without boundaries. I drank heavily through most of my twenties and continued looking for security in relationships, friends, clothes and jobs. All my searching had left me empty, but when I'd found my spiritual side in the New Age movement, I thought I'd really found my life's purpose.

So, why was she bringing up Jesus now? This was not one of our normal conversations. Didn't she know all religions were just a form of cultural worship of God—many paths, one end point? As soon as she left, I reached for my phone to call my business partner and make fun of my friend.

Right then and there, the Holy Spirit fell on me. I realized that, just after claiming I did everything from love, I was preparing to make fun of my friend's beliefs because they weren't mine. The truth broke through. I wasn't love-centered. I was self-centered.

My eyes finally opened. I had been deceived. I wasn't serving a divine god. I was serving the devil himself! I wasn't being blessed by the universe, I was being dragged into hell. The god I served didn't care if I smoked weed. Didn't care if I worshiped myself. Didn't care if I watched pornographic movies, cursed, got drunk, gossiped or lied if it suited me. He didn't even mind if I said all paths lead to God. He wasn't looking for my worship, but my failure. What I'd thought were successes were actually detours leading me away from salvation—away from my rightful place in the kingdom of God Jesus offered me.

From Deception to Discernment

Jesus said, "I am the way, the Truth, and the Life, no one may come to the Father except through me," (John 14:6 NIV). How many times had I heard that verse as a youth? Suddenly, I realized the weight it carried—the weight of Truth. I'd been so sold on *my* truth, I hadn't recognized the Absolute Truth that stands firm regardless of my opinion.

Standing by the phone that day, the spiritual realm I'd followed in my quest for New Age enlightenment came into focus. Its light was anything but pure. Instead, it radiated with demons and an angel of light who came to kill, steal, and destroy.

The counterfeit lay exposed before me, and I began to weep. In a flurry of activity, I grabbed my weed, bongs, pipes, crystals and books on Zen meditation and Eastern philosophy. I threw them all in the garbage. I had been searching for spiritual guidance since that first Tarot card reading. But now I had found the real thing!

I dug out the Bible I'd buried away as a youth and opened it at random. Luke 15:1-7 lay before me. "Suppose one of you has a hundred sheep and loses one of them. Does he not leave the ninety-nine in the open country and go after the lost sheep until he finds it? And when he finds it, he joyfully puts it on his shoulders and goes home. Then he calls his friends and neighbors together and says, 'Rejoice with me; I have found my lost sheep.' I tell you that in the same way there will be more rejoicing in heaven over one sinner who repents than over ninety-nine righteous persons who do not need to repent" (NIV).

I was the one lost sheep!

I was the prodigal who had wandered off into the world!

And I was undone.

I called my sweet, Holy Spirit-filled mom—a woman whose floor was worn out from the prayers and pleading for her daughter's soul. "Get ready for a party, Mom! Your prodigal daughter is coming home!"

Kingdom Takeaway

Romans 12:1-2 is one of my favorite verses. "Therefore, I urge you, brothers and sisters, in view of God's mercy, to offer your bodies as a living sacrifice, holy and pleasing to God—this is your true and proper worship. Do not conform to the pattern of this world, but be transformed by the renewing of your mind. Then you will be able to test and approve what God's will is—his good, pleasing and perfect will," (NIV).

Have you chosen to live life *your* way like I did? As you can see from my story, my way led me down a dark road of bondage. Because I didn't know the Word of God, I fell for all the trappings of the New Age movement. I justified the false religion and compromised God's truth. But when I opened up the Word of God, my mind was transformed, and I found my way home to the Father.

If you have been a prodigal like me, your heavenly Father has been watching for your return. The Good Shepherd has been looking for you. He's not going to scold or punish you. He doesn't look back at where you have come from. He sees where you are going and celebrates your journey.

Laughter Lemonade

By M. Janet Mangum

The joy of the Lord is your strength.

(Nehemiah 8:10 NKJV)

There I was, standing under a tree before forty-some pastors in a foreign country, my face covered with children's stickers and comical green sunglasses. I could hardly believe I was about to offer laughter workshops.

This was not my normal teaching. The team I served with was filled with mighty women of God capable of teaching and preaching on just about any subject. Yet here I was, convinced I had an assignment from God to make these pastors laugh. What was I thinking?

We were ministering in a part of Asia that had been suffering from severe drought, so we fed the attendees of our event for several days. They came by the hundreds and hundreds, along with their whole families. Our leader, Lana, called home to ask her husband to arrange for more funds. That way, we could buy the large amounts of food we needed for the hungry and discouraged families.

Getting Assignments

One member of our team, JoAnne, was a leader of leaders. Knowing this, Lana assigned her to the main auditorium where she could speak to hundreds of ministry leaders. Meanwhile, she sent me to an enormous shade tree where more than forty pastors awaited me.

A welcome breeze fanned us as we sat in the shade. I began the morning session by explaining the medical value of laughter. The very act releases endorphins, our body's natural feel-good chemical, into our bloodstream. It lowers stress levels, burns calories, and quite literally soothes tension in our bodies. Laughing exercises our lungs, heart, diaphragm, and stomach, helping our circulation by clearing toxins from the respiratory system. It's our body's natural antidote for stress, pain and conflict.

Nothing seems to work faster or more dependably than laughter to return our minds and bodies to a healthy balance.

After this, I shared Scriptures confirming the benefits God wants us to gain from it. “He will yet fill your mouth with laughter and your lips with shouting,” (Job 8:21 ESV). “The joy of the Lord is your strength,” (Nehemiah 8:10 NKJV). “The cheerful heart has a continual feast,” (Proverbs 15:15 NIV).

In other words, a good belly roll and deep, overtaking laughter is not only good for us physically and emotionally, but spiritually, as well. It’s a bundle of blessing for our body!

Finally, I talked about my own stories of transforming sadness, worry or depression into relief and laughter. I used props to help explain how I discovered childlike ways to get myself to grin, laugh out loud or just shout with gusto. I pulled out my bulbous orange shoes, large, silly, green sunglasses, a wand from a children’s toy room and large colorful stickers. These had helped me through those times when laughter was the farthest thing from my mind.

Someone was translating all this to the audience for me, but I had trouble reading the looks on their faces. I couldn’t tell how anyone was responding.

At the end of the session, I told them our next meeting would be later that same day, back under this broad-leafed tree. Their assignment was to return with clean jokes to share with the group.

Meanwhile, Uh-Oh!

After dismissing my group, I walked past the large auditorium where JoAnne was just summing up her time with the leaders. Hundreds were on their knees in prayer, tears splashing on the cement floor in front of them. The Holy Spirit was renewing, refreshing and releasing them from the bondage of ministry and family stresses. Each one was having a stunning revelation of God’s heart for them while JoAnne followed the leading of the Holy Spirit moving amongst them. I felt like I had accidentally entered a deeply private session between them and God. I was in awe, to say the least.

As the leaders solemnly left the auditorium and passed me, I began to feel foolish. Here JoAnne was, meeting deep emotional needs, targeting their sacrifices and ministry lives in a dynamic and healthy way. Meanwhile, I'd been talking about laughter while wearing big, silly-looking green sunglasses! What had I just done?

Finishing What I Started

When it was time to go back under that tree and listen to the pastors tell jokes, you can imagine how I felt. I'd totally missed the mark. I was so foolish to think this was God. It was embarrassing, but I had to go finish what I'd started.

I put my big green glasses back on, stuck the children's stickers on my face and donned my fluorescent orange rubber shoes. Then I asked God to forgive me and help me resist embarrassment so I could bring this to a conclusion and just get out of there.

To my surprise, the pastors had followed instructions and came with their jokes. As each one rose to deliver them, I'd say, "Wait! I have to do something to get you and the audience ready." Grinning and winking at the other pastors, I stuck funny children's stickers on the speaker's nose or cheeks. Then I'd run around them a couple times, tap them on the head with my wand, and say, "Ready. Now go!"

It's difficult to describe how silly I got, preparing them to tell their jokes. They were all grown men, pastors of churches and overseers of other pastors. There I was, tapping them on the head with a little wand, covering them with stickers and expecting them to go with the flow of what I was doing.

They began stoically, but as they opened their mouths, the audience responded by roaring with laughter. After the first two presented their jokes, the spectators started laughing before I could even complete my decorations. What a sight we were. What might an observer have thought if they happened to pass by?

The pastors told their jokes in their own language. My interpreter, not wanting to see me left out, tried translating the jokes into English for me. Now, humor is different in different cultures. What was funny to the pastors was an enigma to me.

I didn't want them to be disappointed, so I practiced my laugh-on-purpose, rip-roaring, belly-rolling demonstration. It was my usual tactic for getting myself to laugh through difficult times whether the situation called for it or not.

The workshops lasted about an hour and a half each. When I finished, I was completely spent. I took my big funny glasses and went over to where the children gathered and played with them. Though my sessions had been a success, I still felt despondent. I was sure I had missed the Holy Spirit's leading and just hoped my silly workshop hadn't embarrassed my leader, Lana.

Surprise, Surprise.

My interpreter turned out to be the vice-president of a denomination and had several churches himself. You can imagine what I thought he'd have to say when he asked to talk with me after dinner.

Our conversation began soberly. He explained that laughter isn't acceptable in ministry settings in his culture. It was considered frivolous and disrespectful for many reasons. At home or with close friends, they would laugh and tell clean jokes, but never in a setting like the one we were in together.

He went on to say he had come to the conference with every intention of stepping down from his position when it was over. Trying times were making it too difficult to continue in this role and still take care of his family. While interpreting the sessions, he found himself laughing over and over at me and my silly props and all the jokes. He felt the weight of depression lift away as he soaked in the humor.

The experience had both healed and delivered him from emotional bondage. He no longer had to carry a heavy load while being spiritually drained. Because of what the Holy Spirit had done during our times together, he realized he could remain in his position and serve after all.

Not only that, but he wanted me to do it again! He wanted another group of leaders to experience freedom and healing from the laughter workshops.

I did. We did. But most of all, God did!

Kingdom Takeaway

Whoever coined the phrase, *Laughter is the best medicine* probably didn't realize it was a Biblical statement, as well. Laughter is a gift from God. Job 8:21 says He even fills our mouths with it.

Maybe you could use some lighthearted tools against the effects of hard work or frustrating circumstances this very day. Proverbs 15:15 describes a merry heart as having a continual feast. While desperate pleas or heartbroken tears are appropriate some days, the value of a merry heart with a good belly laugh can't be overlooked.

I thank God for the validation I received that day. Had I continued comparing what I thought I heard from God to what others had heard that day, the experience could have spoken negatively into my life. Instead, God intervened with unexpected grace—the Holy Spirit showing Himself strong to meet the heartfelt needs of His leaders.

You may not have had all your experiences validated the way mine were. But I often say, "Give it your best shot prayerfully and obediently." Remain teachable, and trust that God has a plan. If by chance you did truly miss it somehow, He will turn it around for good. As the old saying (sort of) goes, "Let God turn your lemons to lemonade."

From Victim to Weapon

By Anonymous

As told to JoAnne Meckstroth

Learning to let go is not giving up!
It is simply passing the burden to a better fighter (God)
so you can fight another day.

—Shannon L. Alder

We were an average American family living the good life, a loving couple with five adult children ranging from ages twenty-eight to nineteen. We were hardworking, law-abiding citizens with strong Christian ethics.

And then, the unthinkable happened.

Our beautiful daughter became trapped in the dark web of human sex trafficking. She was groomed, branded and beaten. For over three years now, she's been sent out to have sex for money. The trauma has nearly ripped our family apart.

Sex trafficking is real. Horrific. Evil. Sadly, I am only one of many mothers and fathers living a similar nightmare. It isn't one you soon wake up from—it can take months or even years, depending on how quickly your loved one can be rescued.

I'm sharing my story to help you understand the signs to look for in your own children and to challenge you to get involved and fight back with me against this evil.

A Dubious Friend Appears

My daughter (I'll call her JJ) was bright, energetic, compassionate and fun to be around as she was growing up. She blossomed into a beautiful young woman with one of the sweetest, most caring personalities. Her huge heart had her dreaming of becoming a missionary traveling the world to help children who were hungry, trafficked and homeless.

She was also an artist and wanted to be a photographer and entrepreneur like her mama. She looked for the good in people and trusted them to be as kind and honest as she was. She was my innocent lamb.

JJ finished high school a year ahead of her class and started taking courses at the community college. Although only seventeen, she seemed to flourish in her new environment. We talked often, sometimes yakking about nothing for hours.

Then one day she told me about her new friend.

"Mom, I've met this really shy guy. His name is Jeremy. I don't think he has a good family life and I've been helping him out. I feel sorry for him." Apparently, he often spent nights on friends' couches because he dreaded going home to the smell of alcohol and his parents' fights.

My brow wrinkled, but JJ tried to reassure me. "Come on, Mom. He doesn't sleep on *my* couch. I just give him rides. It's the right thing to do."

When I finally met Jeremy, I was immediately suspicious. I told JJ, "Please be careful, I don't have a good feeling about this boy."

"Oh Mama, you're such a worry wart. He just needs a good friend."

I couldn't shake my concerns, but over time, I began questioning myself. How could I judge this boy without really knowing him? Maybe I was just anxious because JJ was growing up.

Instincts Prove Right

I worried as JJ's phone calls and visits gradually became less frequent. Then one day she came home to spend a night in her old bedroom. At first, it was like old times. We talked, laughed and watched our favorite movies together.

But, about two o'clock in the morning, her phone rang.

I heard her say, "I'll be right there," and hurried to the front door to stop her. I wasn't about to let her go by herself. We'd be taking my car and I would be driving.

At the rendezvous point, Jeremy jumped out of the shadows and into my back seat. A thick, oppressive spirit squeezed in right alongside of him. He was nervous. I was nervous. If he had made one wrong move, I would have wrestled that boy down to the ground like a ferocious mama bear.

After we dropped him off, I had a serious conversation with JJ about this relationship. At last, she confessed he *had* been acting strange recently and she promised to stop helping him. A few months later, she moved away from the area (and Jeremy) and I breathed a sigh of relief. The threat was surely over.

When she returned home within the year, my anxiety level shot back up. The timing couldn't have been worse. My husband and I were just packing up to move to another state. She'd be moving back to Jeremy's territory with no one around to watch over her.

As hard as it was to leave her, I still felt I needed to let JJ go. She was in her early twenties, after all. It was time to let her find her own path in life.

Distance Becomes a Problem

It wouldn't be long before geography wasn't the only thing putting distance between us. JJ pulled away from us emotionally, spiritually and mentally, as well. If we tried to talk with her about her personal life, she pushed back or simply avoided talking with us.

"I'll call you later, Mom," she'd say. But the phone never rang.

Even when I tried visiting her in person, I sensed a difference in her. She looked okay. She said all the right words. But she wouldn't let our conversations go below the surface. Wondering what she was hiding, I prayed with a new level of intensity when I got home.

What a surprise when, months later, she called asking to come home.

"Of course you can come back, JJ! When?"

"Right now!"

She tried to put on a good face when she arrived, but the change in her was unmistakable. JJ was no longer the confident and vivacious young woman I had raised. She was preoccupied, on edge and low in self-esteem. What could have happened to make her so ashamed?

Even though she continued to resist questions about her personal life, it was good to have her living close by. We often shared dinner and she started working in my boutique. It seemed to be a place where she could flourish and blossom. Sometimes she even appeared to be happy.

Crises Are Never Convenient

When a crisis hits your family, it doesn't care what other challenges you might be experiencing. I was helping my best friend's family deal with her pending death and was so focused on it, I barely noticed JJ was withdrawing again. Worse still, unbeknownst to me, she was in the final stage of being groomed into human sex trafficking.

Two weeks after I buried my friend, JJ told me she was moving to Costa Rica—with Jeremy. His name washed over me like an ice-cold, bone-chilling shower.

"We've been in touch for some time now. His uncle lives in Costa Rica and is going to help pay for our trip. I'll be working on a plant farm and Jeremy will take a job in his uncle's medical clinic."

I begged her to not go, but it didn't matter.

"Mom, I'm leaving in three days. I didn't tell you and Dad earlier because I knew you'd be upset."

Getting Educated

My husband and I were frantic. We called our friend, an undercover narcotics agent in our hometown, and asked if he could look up Jeremy's name.

He went silent for a moment. "I don't have to. His file is sitting on my partner's desk. He's been in and out of jail for theft, stabbing and drugs. He's a trafficker of many things. You must convince your daughter to not go with him. He took his last victim to Mexico and traded her to the cartel for a supply of heroin." The cartel had threatened to kill her family if she spoke out. Afraid for their safety, the girl refused to press charges so the authorities couldn't touch him.

Sadly, this is the pattern of most cartel victims—if they survive.

"Oh my God," we moaned. "How in the world could this have happened?"

"He's most likely been grooming your daughter for some time and possibly drugging her without her even knowing it."

Using Every Tool

We had to change JJ's mind before she left the country, so we sprang into action.

A narcotics intervention group gave us advice and support. The Federal Bureau of Investigation offices exchanged information. Even a friend found a way to help. She happened to stop by a local coffee shop and saw JJ with a man she didn't recognize. She snapped a photo and sent it to me. It was Jeremy, ready to pick her up!

When JJ came to say goodbye to us, my husband and an intervention team were waiting to talk with her. But she refused to believe the truth, turned her back and closed the door behind her. That was over three years ago. We haven't seen her since.

We know she never made it to Costa Rica. The FBI had warned Jeremy to not leave the country, so he took her to another major sex trafficking hub in Florida instead. Since then, JJ has rarely been able to contact us. When she does call, it's only for a minute or so. "Hey, Mama, it's me, JJ." My heart pounds—she's alive! I quickly tell her how much Dad and I love her and we're ready to come get her. I remind her there is nothing Jesus can't heal.

Between sobs, she whispers, "I love you" and is gone again.

Battle Weary

I miss having JJ in my life. I miss her funny phone messages, her giddy laugh, our dinners together, our movie nights and the love we share. I long to hear her say, "Mom, come get me!" My husband and I keep our cell phones nearby just in case she calls, and we have extra cash on hand for last minute airline tickets.

Meanwhile, I cope with an inconsolable pain that beats against my soul and challenges my sanity. When this all started, I struggled to get out of bed. I couldn't stop imagining my daughter high on drugs and being stripped of her human identity—or worse. Utter despondency often led me to a frantic impulse to do something—anything. I feared she may die, leaving a permanent crack on my soul.

Battle Cry

After three years of living this nightmare, the pain has not lessened, but I've turned my grief and fear into a battle cry.

Psalms 37:5–6 says it all. "Commit everything you do to the Lord. Trust Him and He will help you. He will make your innocence radiate like the dawn, and the justice of your cause will shine like the noonday sun," (NLT).

I am no longer a victim. I am God's weapon! I fight for justice and have partnered with a statewide organization that educates and brings public awareness of these violent acts against our children and our society. My story will never be a deep, dark secret in our family because I take every opportunity to share.

I pray and stand in the gap for marriages. This kind of trauma brings tremendous stress into relationships. It will either tear a marriage apart or bind it together. My husband and I have gone through both. Today, we are united in the fight. We pray together, cry together and prepare together.

Be thoughtful of a parent's pain in this situation because it's impossible to hide. For me, it's a raw pain without words—the sadness in my eyes, the slope of my shoulders, the deep frown lines that don't seem to leave even when I smile. Some friends weep openly and pray with me. Others don't want to hear the horrors I've gone through and avoid me. Some question my story. After all, this kind of thing only happens in other countries and in the movies, right? And of course, there are the unspoken judgments about what my husband and I must have done wrong as parents.

Difficult Duty

I challenge every parent to be bold. As uncomfortable as it may be, talk to your kids about human sex trafficking, and include them in creating a strategy—a plan of escape. Have emergency phone numbers on speed dial. Talk about different scenarios and ways they might stay out of trouble. If possible, take them to a self-defense course to learn the fundamentals of self-protection and survival.

Help your children discover their God-given identity and strengths, to become strong decision makers and to understand God's unconditional love.

Professional traffickers look for the weak and vulnerable areas when grooming their victims. Sometimes they are groomed for several years until they can control them. Other victims are randomly snatched off the streets.

Kingdom Challenge

Will you join me in the fight? Every day, in every city, sex trafficking and pedophilia reach into the very fabric of our culture. These heinous crimes are likely already in your neighborhood preparing to knock on your door.

You may feel frozen because no amount of action seems to be enough. But everyone can do something. First and foremost, pray for truth to be revealed about trafficking issues in the United States. Support those who are actively fighting this war. They have stepped into the dirtiest, darkest and most demonic atmospheres imaginable. Our prayers and encouragement will keep them strong.

Finally, become an activist. Find out what anti-trafficking efforts are being made in your state, city and church. Then fill in the gap with your gifts and natural talents.

Become a weapon in the hand of God and join me in the fight.

As you do, remember: Satan is no longer *your* enemy—you are *his*!

The Power in Your Yes

By Lecia Retter

Stop praying, "Use me," and pray, "Make me useable."

—Reinhard Bonnke

I heard the Holy Spirit whisper, "Lecia…Lecia…your success is in your *yes*."

Looking back, I can see how my *yes* has become a pillar—a stake in the ground. It's something I have striven to carry out in my walk with God.

The journey to yes, however, has been complex. I've had to upgrade my faith, push through fear and take a few risks. It wasn't easy because life had strengthened fear's foothold in me. The enemy wanted to emotionally paralyze me and spiritually neutralize me.

But I had Romans 12:2. "And do not be conformed to this world, but be transformed by the renewing of your mind, that you may prove what is that good and acceptable and perfect will of God," (NKJV). Over time, my faith in Christ transformed my mind and He empowered me to tear down every stronghold the enemy attempted to erect. The Holy Spirit gave me the courage to say *no* to fear and *yes* to the unknown.

Fear Comes Calling

The real journey to freedom began over a decade ago while attending a School of Ministry class on dreams. We were sharing our dreams of partnering with God to change the world. The more I listened to the other students, though, the more insignificant and useless I felt. (I was "sportin' a 'tude," as my husband and I said to our girls when they had a bad attitude.)

Participating in these dream sessions seemed to shove open a door to fear I thought I had closed long ago.

I had vivid images of God closing this door. (I could still hear the sound of the guillotine crashing over it as the flow of Jesus' blood sealed the door to fear shut.) Though I knew it was a lie that this door was opening, it still bothered me.

My mom used to say, "If you don't have anything nice to say, don't say anything at all." So, as another week of sharing and teaching went on, I kept my mouth sealed shut. But that didn't keep me from going outside to whine and complain to Jesus during class breaks.

"Jesus, I need you to redefine who I am," I finally prayed. "I'm not budging from this place until you do. I need a greater understanding of who you say I am. I need a deeper revelation of the dreams you have placed within me." I knew it was impossible for fear to thrive if I was secure in my godly purpose and identity. My relationship with the Lord was simply too valuable to allow that door to reopen.

The Answers Begin

During one of my many complaint sessions, Jesus interrupted me with several questions.

"What breaks your heart that breaks mine?"

Without hesitation I said, "Sex-trafficking." The issue had been on my mind for a couple of years by then.

"How many thirty-minute segments are in a year?"

What an odd question for Him to ask. Surely, He knew. I whipped out my cell phone calculator and answered. "17,520."

Now, issues like trafficking can feel overwhelming. The numbers are staggering, involving an estimated minimum of forty million people—the equivalent of the state of California or the population of metro Tokyo! But the thought God had downloaded made me pause.

"What if we *could* change the outcome in the battle against trafficking by praying and supporting this war in heaven while others here on earth rescued those enslaved?" Such a simple idea, but I felt excitement grow in me. "What if we *could* be effective? What would we do if God wiped out all our excuses and replaced them with two simple requirements? You must believe in Jesus and believe in the power of prayer."

Vision and purpose collided within me. I knew what to do. I would gather people to pray, allowing the power of united, focused intercession to become the tipping point which would bring an end to sex-trafficking.

If only 17,520 people prayed for an end to trafficking for thirty minutes during a single year, they could cover this violent issue in prayer twenty-four hours a day, seven days a week. If those same people donated $1.00 for each minute of prayer to an anti-trafficking organization, they could supply $525,600 to the frontlines of the battle every year!

I've found what Paul wrote in Ephesians 3:20 to really be true. God achieves infinitely more than our greatest request, our most unbelievable dream and our wildest imagination.

What Do You Do With a Dream?

What should we do when a dream is born or we have a prophetic word? I can tell you what Joseph did. In Genesis 37–45, we see his story filled with the highest of hopes and the deepest lows of despair. Through it all, his faith and *yes* to God never wavered.

Sold into slavery at a young age, Joseph was accused unjustly by Potiphar's wife and thrown into prison for years. When he interpreted the dreams of two fellow prisoners, he thought his release would soon follow. Instead, he was forgotten and barely survived in the dark, foul-smelling, rat-infested dungeon. At long last, Pharoah asked Joseph to interpret *his* dream and years of imprisonment came to an end. Joseph spent the rest of his days in the palace, second in command to Pharoah.

Dreams Take Time

For eight long years, my cycles of highs and lows seemed to mirror Joseph's.

About nine months after God gave me the dream, I felt a brief but strong sense of urgency. "Do it now! Do it right now!" Though I tried to bring it to life, I lacked the skills to move forward. The dream seemed to fizzle.

Soon, God pointed me toward a specific ministry group who focused on prophetic intercession, writing crafted prayers and developing an identity statement.

For several years, this apparent detour became a training ground for skills I needed. I learned to see myself the way God sees me—discovered who He says I am.

Still, the yearning continued. "God use me! Send me! Increase my capacity to love like You do! Increase my ability to receive Your love!" As my inner self transformed, God provided opportunities to grow into my identity.

One of the most significant began with my husband. The Holy Spirit downloaded a message to him while he was at work. "Tell Lecia she has authority in the areas I have given her. Let there be no doubt. I will see to it that you accomplish all that I have established in your hearts. Do not doubt. Do not fear. I will open the doors. You have no way to know how it will happen. It will come quickly. It will come swiftly. I will see to it you have all you need. I am an equipper of good things. My children never lack. No fear. No fear. No fear."

Three days after he shared this with me, I received an invitation to travel with a team of women to the Philippines as an intercessor. Our team leader suggested I come with a couple of sermons in my pocket—just in case. Her "just in case" worried me a bit because I had little speaking experience.

I made a crucial decision on the long airplane ride to Manilla. I told her, "I'm going to give you my *yes* now. I am sure I'll be in situations where I will want to say no, but you already have my *yes*!" I've since said the same thing to the Lord. "My answer to You will always be an emphatic *yes*!"

What Can *Yes* Bring?

Did my *yes* mean the cycles of hope and discouragement ended? No.

In 2013, a conference speaker challenged us to ask ourselves this question: "What kind of person do you need to become to see your word fulfilled?" As mentioned earlier, it took eight long years between the vision and the evidence of something being built. During those years my life was filled with struggles and opportunities. Every high and low experience taught me to grow in trust and boldness and to stand firm on the fact God would be faithful.

On a Sunday morning in 2019, I remembered a vision told to me by a friend five years earlier. She had seen a steel trap door on the ground. Dark, dirty, filthy arms in shackles and chains clawed at the door trying to open it. Suddenly a red woman's shoe (like the ruby slipper in the Wizard of Oz) held the door open, letting the light of heaven shine into the darkness. The chains fell off the prisoners and they emerged clean and free.

I'd known right away the shoe had symbolized me as a Kansas native. That day in the conference, the vision flooded back to me. I could hear the screams of those imprisoned and I began to cry and travail in prayer. A concerned friend came over and joined me. As I shared my thoughts, she began to smile. "My daughter works for a marketing agency who helps one nonprofit each year. You should call her.

Breaking Through Fear

This was the first of many doors which began to open as the vision came into being. I entered each door with hesitant footsteps. Again and again, the enemy attempted to rebuild a wall of fear to stop me.

For one thing, I had to embrace and overcome my embarrassment about my lack of technological skills. Each time I confronted the wall by openly confessing my ignorance and asking for help, I kicked a hole in the barrier of fear. With each hole I kicked in, God opened another door, and I stepped across threshold after threshold of uncertainty.

One day I was trying to line up a marketing intern to help me. The university where I work politely informed me I would have to possess some marketing skills of my own before I could have an intern. They had no marketing volunteers waiting in the wings to assist me, so I was sent on my way.

I was barely back in my office before my phone rang. A student had suddenly appeared right after I'd left. She announced she'd be leaving the next morning to work for an anti-trafficking organization in Asia. I connected with her immediately and shared my dream of gathering people to pray against sex-trafficking. It wasn't long before she commented, "By myself I don't feel I can accomplish much but combined with so many other people praying, I could make a difference." Our conversation clarified and confirmed my passion.

Trafficking is the target, but my zeal is for the body of Christ to recognize the power of united prayer. Our unity will reveal Jesus to the world!

Another threshold I had to step over came the day God told me to join a departmental book club. We were studying a book I had no desire to read. After we made introductions, I realized why God wanted me there. Almost every other member of the group was in the marketing department! One of them would eventually become our main marketing partner and avid supporter.

Over the course of several months, we founded our UP (Unstoppable Prayer) Movement. Students designed the website for our nonprofit. Donations came in to meet our needs and we began the process of signing people up to pray.

We still have cycles of hope and discouragement, yet we are always aware of God's faithful guidance. And, as I often remind Him, "This is Your deal, God. You said 17,520 people and I trust You to bring them." Our partnership is solid, and He has my emphatic *yes*!

Kingdom Takeaway

Reinhart Bonnke was right when he said, "Stop praying, 'Use me' and pray, 'Make me useable,'" Every time we say *yes* to God, we are also agreeing to allow Him to make us useable. Our *yes* gives the Holy Spirit permission to uncover false limitations and fears life may have built into us. Our *yes* brings us internal freedom and makes us more useable for His kingdom purposes.

Take a moment and ask what you may be capable of doing when you say *yes* to uniting with others in prayer? I invite you to be one of the people necessary to fulfill the UP Movement's goal of praying to end trafficking and let the enslaved go free. (https://upmovement.org)

Everyday Miracles

By Melanie Boudreau

We won't be perfect on this side of heaven. But Jesus is perfect. Always.
We are becoming more holy and true. Jesus already is. His name isn't "Becoming." It is "I Am." Perfection isn't the goal. Jesus is.

—Stasi Eldredge, *Becoming Myself: Embracing God's Dream of You*

I have one job this morning—to get my grandchildren to school on time. My daughter left a careful list of instructions that spelled it out clearly.

"Leave the house by 7:15 AM."

I am clever. I remember the ordeal a simple task of loading the car with small children can be. We step out the door at 7:00 AM sharp with me thinking fifteen minutes to load should be ample.

Silly me. It's been too long. I should have started at 3:00 AM.

The Boston terrier escapes when the door opens. No big deal. She usually self-potties and runs back to the door—unless there is a raccoon in the yard. Pup Olive took off like a bat out of hell, disappearing into the Tennessee woods. The children follow in hot pursuit, but to no avail. They're impressed how their skittish dog penetrates the forest without reserve.

Then it's my turn. Leash in hand, into the woods I go. I spot Olive's quarry precariously teetering on a branch over our heads. Eventually, I manage to corral our domesticated crazed beast. I coax her out of the brush and back into civilization.

Enough adventure for one day. These kids must get to school!

With children in their car seats and I behind the wheel, I press the ignition.

"Key fob not found."

This is a push button ignition, and the fob is clearly in my hand. Okay, I reason, there is an emergency manual key hidden in every fob. I extract it and look for the insertion slot. Dashboard? No. Under the cup holder? No. In the storage bay? No. Dash again? By my knees? No and no.

Ugh!

My grandson, Brave, mentions the penalties levied against him for arriving late to homeroom at the start of the day.

Fortunately, my quick-thinking beloved searches Google for "Mazda Fob Reset" and gets the vehicle to respond. Off we go! Thank you, Grandpa!

Now, we live in Colorado, but we're babysitting in Nashville. I don't know my way around, but I am quick with my GPS and am equipped with the address of the children's school preloaded. Arriving at the first spaghetti-like junction, the default program presents options that don't match the road signs. Nashville roads can have four different names, but only a local will know which names aren't listed on the overhead sign. And I am no local.

Pulling off in heavy traffic, I switch programs and the alternate navigation application chooses a route that actually matches the signage. How was I to know it would be a fifteen-minute diversion to loop back around? And loop we do.

I pray for a miracle—an immediate teleportation which would somehow pull us into the car line right on time. That particular miracle does not happen. My grandchildren are late to school this morning—my first day behind the wheel of parenting them. The first day my daughter and her husband had entrusted me with their precious lives.

Other miracles had taken place, however—ones which had taken a number of years to develop. The first miracle was remaining calm under pressure. The next was not giving in to shame after failure. I was also able to see humor in circumstances in real time, even though the outcome threatened to make me look bad.

He's also produced a miraculous capacity to just be present and love life.

I am connected to the God of the universe who smiles at me as I navigate life. With Him, I'm able to just be present and love life—to love well in the midst of stress. His indwelling presence, coupled with the fruit of His Spirit, causes my character to reflect His, in greater and greater ways.

Growing a Miracle

These miracles didn't suddenly appear. They were planted like seeds within me when I was reconciled to God through the death of Christ. He brought me into His presence and stood me up blameless before God. Since then, His Spirit within me continues to progressively make me holy, day by day.

This miracle is in each of us because Christ lives in us! The Passion Translation puts it this way: "There is a divine mystery—a secret surprise that has been concealed from the world for generations, but now it's being revealed, unfolded and manifested for every holy believer to experience. Living within you is the Christ who floods you with the expectation of glory! This mystery of Christ, embedded within us, becomes a heavenly treasure chest of hope filled with the riches of glory for his people, and God wants everyone to know it!" (Colossians 1:26-27 TPT)

It reminds me of being pregnant with my first child. I could sense another life within my body. As a new mother, I knew this life was present whether I could feel my baby moving or she remained still. In a similar way, we are the dwelling place of God (1 Corinthians 3:16). Christ dwells in us *perpetually*, no matter how we feel in the midst of life's trials.

Expectation

Because of the power—the Person—I possessed within me, I've learned to envision and expect the things that happened when Christ was physically present upon this earth. I expect oppression to lift, storms to calm, peace to prevail, demons to flee, miracles to happen, healings to occur and truth to prevail.

We can experience these outcomes today because if He lives in us, He is wherever we are. With confidence and joy, we know He comes with us into our circumstances, or into the darkness. As He does, He envelopes those He loves and expands the reach of His kingdom.

Kingdom Takeaway

Right now, while you are struggling with your circumstances, Christ is in you, releasing His supernatural peace and causing you to advance in faith. Will you, in the midst of a challenging day, receive His provision in the person of His presence and watch the same miraculous fruit of His presence unfold?

The Spirit of God has made His permanent home in us! What a miracle to have His indwelling presence—daily provision for a lifetime.

Freedom

By M. Janet Mangum

But if I cast out demons by the Spirit of God, surely the kingdom of God has come upon you.

(Matthew 12:28 NLT)

"Janet, I am desperate. Can I come over for prayer?"

Mariana, a young friend, often called asking for prayer. She had continual bouts with confusion and desperation. Even quality therapists had been unable to find the cause of her tormented condition. Nothing either she or her therapists had tried seemed to make a difference.

I didn't know what I could accomplish that the experts could not, but I was willing to petition our heavenly Father once more on her behalf. Little did I realize how different the result would be this time—all because I had met a woman named Kathy recently at a Bible study.

Kathy had taken me aside at one point to whisper, "God asked me to talk to you about deliverance." I wasn't sure what she meant by this, but we made plans to meet for lunch and discuss it further. In the restaurant, she talked about setting people free from evil influences that may be tormenting. She shared some basic principles about the spirit realm.

Oh, how basic they were!

- God is good.
- The devil is bad.
- Both have messengers.
- Jesus is the powerful name that is the answer.
- Forgiveness is a key.
- Don't be afraid.

"You will need this," Kathy said, "or He wouldn't have told me to tell you. When you meet someone in this situation, call me. I will come to pray for them."

The Holy Spirit was evident in her life, so I firmly believed her message was from God. "How will I know what to look for?" I asked.

"You won't miss it. Just call me."

It was days, or maybe a week later, when Mariana asked for prayer. As soon as I opened the door to her, she began acting strangely. Her voice went up and down in volume and tone. Her body language unnerved me, and she kept crying out, "My flesh is on fire!" She seemed totally incoherent.

Nevertheless, I invited her inside. As she sat on my couch, it became clear. Mariana was one of *those* people Kathy had been talking about, so I called her immediately. She told me to sit quietly with Mariana and pray softly in my spiritual language (referred to as tongues in the Bible). "At all times," she warned, "do not show fear! I will be right there."

Mariana started verbally threatening me. In various voice tones, she vehemently repeated, "Stop praying like that!" I endeavored with all my might not to show fear or give any indication of how clueless I felt about what to do.

Thankfully, Kathy arrived quickly. The second she entered the door, Mariana stilled. She suddenly became her normal self and greeted Kathy with a sweet "Hello."

Now what? I wondered. *Kathy will think I am exaggerating*. I took her aside to the kitchen for a minute. "Honest, she was acting very weird just a few minutes ago."

"I know," Kathy replied, "she needs freedom. The spirits of darkness who have tormented her for so long know you are new at this. They also know I am confident in my identity in Jesus, and that my Lord and I have had years of experience casting out devils. Their only hope is to scare you into sending her home and to hide from me. Watch and pray. You will see their tyranny is over. The kingdom of God is here."

My role for the evening was to observe and pray softly while Kathy addressed the spiritual needs of my young friend—forgiveness from the sinful behaviors in which she'd been engaging.

Mariana repented of her past and gave her life to Jesus that evening with no interruption from evil spirits. She not only asked Jesus to forgive her, but willingly forgave all those who had harmed her or misled her in any way.

Her freedom gave me a spectacular view into the glory of God—announcing His kingdom on earth on behalf of those bound by evil spirits. As each of the now powerless demonic presences left Mariana, I watched her body twist and turn in unfathomable ways. After an hour or so, Mariana sat quietly, exhausted, but calm and smiling, completely free and deeply thankful. Through it all, I saw how much more powerful Jesus's name was than anyone or anything I could imagine!

I marveled at how many times I had believed Jesus is the way, the truth and the life and yet hadn't had a clue about the depth of the authority He has given us. Nor had I comprehended the level of access into the kingdom of God on earth He gives us to result in God's glory and the demons' defeat!

Since that first experience, the Holy Spirit has sent thousands bound by evil spirits my way for freedom. Some of them came with friends and some alone. They all came to understand their needs were strongly influenced by evil spirits but didn't know how to access freedom in Christ Jesus.

I have had the honor of watching the power of Jesus's name glorify God in dramatic and beautiful ways. Freedom is a gift from Him! Jesus said he came to destroy the works of darkness (1 John 1:8).

The presence of God has been evident in sweet and powerful expressions of the Holy Spirit—both for the ones praying as well as those desperately searching for His life-giving freedom. At the close of each session, we invite the Holy Spirit to fill all the spaces the enemy was held captive. We invite refreshment and healing to invade the souls that had so long been tormented. Smiles, hugs and often hilarious laughter break out as we celebrate the gift of life together in Him.

Kingdom Takeaway

After my first experience watching demons flee, I sat quietly that evening reading Luke 11:20. “But if I cast out demons with the finger of God, surely the kingdom of God has come upon you,” (NIV).

I couldn’t help but marvel at how merciful and loving my Lord is. When I asked the Holy Spirit to give a simple understanding of what it means to use the word *kingdom*, here’s what came to mind:

It’s more than a what—it’s a *Who*!

It's His presence. His power. It's You!

It's Him—His rule—His reign.

It’s His goodness, His glory—your gain.

It's hope, The Way, and reward.

It's Jesus Christ where and when He is Lord.

Consider praying Mark 16:17 with a heart filled with confidence in the power of the name of Jesus. “And these signs shall follow them that believe; In my name shall they cast out devils; they shall speak with new tongues,” (KJV).

Be a Gumby

By Reneé Duncan

I am always doing things I can't do. That is how I get to do them.

—Pablo Picasso

I admit it—I am a child of the sixties and seventies.

Phew! I feel a load off my shoulders. It is said, "Confession is good for the soul." It must be true, for I feel pretty good.

The years encompassing the sixties and seventies were interesting. Among other things, I have fond memories of one of my favorite toys of the era—Gumby!

Yep, that little stretchable, flexible, green figurine whose friend was an orange horse named Pokey. There was something special about them. They were Claymation characters created in the 1950s and were television celebrities.

Gumby was a flexible toy. I could mold him any way I desired and shape him into whatever I wanted him to be. He was my adjustable companion—flexibility personified.

I think one of the reasons I liked Gumby was because of my mom. She was a godly woman who always wanted to do whatever God wanted her to. Mom taught us the value of being flexible in ministry. At a moment's notice, my siblings and I were required to fulfill the Scripture of 2 Timothy 4:2. "Preach the word! *Be ready in season and out of season,*" (NKJV).

I tried to convince her this Scripture was only talking about preaching and teaching, but she'd have none of that. "It applies to everything. Just do it."

So, we did.

Flexibility would one day become my *motus operandi* in ministry. It provided the answer to many challenges over the years.

Out of a Comfort Zone

As a young adult, I had the opportunity to travel to a South American country to help in the construction of a Bible school building. I was the youngest woman of all of them and extremely green around the gills.

We'd busied ourselves all week trying to complete the finishing work on the sanctuary and dining hall. When the final full day of work rolled around, I suddenly found myself the only one from my team still in the sanctuary. The rest of them had moved down to the dining hall and I felt abandoned. (In my teammates' defense, my presence, at least ten years younger than the rest, most likely felt like an irritant.)

Shortly after realizing I'd been abandoned, the leader returned and asked me to lead and direct the locals. Surprised yet secretly encouraged, I said *yes*. I had been trained by Momma to submit to my leaders and do as they asked, even if I didn't feel adequate for the assignment.

Without reason, however, my initial gratitude quickly morphed into feelings of being placated, rejected and misunderstood. Loneliness sent my mind into overdrive as a voice echoed in my head.

"No one wants me around."

"I don't fit in with the rest of them."

"Why am I even here? I haven't even had opportunity to introduce one person to Christ!"

"I'm such a failure!"

"I must have done something wrong."

After suffering through two parental divorces in my lifetime, I struggled with rejection. Satan decided this would be an opportune moment to beat me down to size and convince me I was a waste of time. I wanted to have a pity party, but God wouldn't allow it. He soon made short work of my little self-focused mood.

Flexibility Proves Useful

I found myself alone and in charge of a challenging situation. We didn't have anything with which to finish sanding the walls.

The tools had all been taken downstairs. I looked at the people around me and could just hear them thinking, "Great. Now what are we supposed to do?"

God gently reminded me He had prepared me for this. (Of course, I argued with him. Imagine. Me! Squabbling with the God of the Universe. Cheeky and foolish!)

At last, I pulled myself together. "Fine, God," I said, none too humbly. "How did you prepare me for this?"

Here's what He said. "*Be instant in season and out of season. This is part of the training I planned long ago for you to receive. For with My calling comes a need for you to follow My direction at a moment's notice. My calling is upon those who are willing to redirect themselves into areas of discomfort and to be flexible in the immediate moment. It is upon those who are willing to ask Me how to do what they need to do in each situation, then to listen and obey.*"

"But God, it isn't fair."

"*Really, Reneé? You are going to use that one?*"

"Well, it's true! How am I supposed to communicate with these people and to complete the job? It's impossible. *And,* I might add, we haven't got any tools with which to do it."

"*To whom is it impossible? Me? Haven't I commanded you to be strong and have courage even in the face of obstacles? Have you asked Me how to do it or are you just going to surrender and pout?*"

That made me pause. "Right. Okay. Then how do I solve this problem?"

We had no sandpaper to smooth the concrete walls and I didn't have an interpreter. There were approximately twenty locals all waiting for me to lead them. I whispered a prayer and soon the Holy Spirit gave me an idea.

I looked around the barren room to see if anything was usable. Nothing. Then I looked outside the exit door and noticed a pile of sawed-off lumber pieces. I picked one up and realized they were very rough on the end.

"This just might work," I thought.

And it did.

So, with a little flexibility and a whole lot of Holy Spirit guidance, we sanded the whole inside wall with pieces of wood.

Booyah!

Take that, Satan!

God Takes Care of Another Complaint

We were almost finished with the assignment and had a little over two hours until we were to leave for the airport. A man walked into my work area who obviously wanted to sell his goods. They dangled from his arms as he came up to me, the only white woman. He probably though I'd be likely to purchase his homemade merchandise.

When I looked at him, I heard the Lord say, "*I brought him here for you. What are you going to do*?"

I quickly formulated an idea. "I will look at your merchandise," I said, "if you will let me share something of great importance with you." He shook his head. I pushed a little more. "It will only take ten minutes. I promise you will want to hear it." After a bit of back and forth—with him trying to sell what he had and me, well, I also had something for him—he finally agreed. I quickly found an interpreter and, ten minutes later, I celebrated a new believer in Christ.

As he prayed with me, I looked up to see an elderly man and a young adult worker crying. Later, I discovered they were his family. They had been praying for many years for him to receive salvation.

God had heard my heart. He knew what would get my blood pumping! He had ordained this moment in time for a soul to join his family in service to Jesus. If I had refused to be flexible, remained in my own little comfort zone and tantrum, I would have missed being a part of an answered prayer. And this man may not have come to Christ.

Incredible!

Time to Ditch the Comfort Zone

Neale Donald Walsch once said, "Life begins at the end of your comfort zone."

Refusing to leave what's comfortable and resisting flexibility stunts our spiritual growth and blinds our spiritual eyes. God is calling us to alter our comfort zones in this new season and respond to the Holy Spirit. Gone is the luxury to do things the way we have always done them, to make one slow move at a time. God wants us to know His character through intimacy with Him, to respond in an instant to His beckoning. When we know Him intimately, and we know His Word closely, we will recognize His voice instantly.

I believe God is giving us assignments uniquely designed to match this new era. They will be different. They will stretch us. They will require trust, obedience, flexibility and an immediate response. If we're quick to answer, the Holy Spirit will engulf us in a *moving comfort zone* of His own creation. I hear Him say, "*Know me, know my Character, know my Word, know my voice and obey now*! *As you step out, I will confirm each step.*"

Jesus has taken me crashing through many comfort zones. With each breakthrough, He brought new levels of His spiritual gifts, opportunities and anointing. Once I adjusted to the new normal, He would switch things up. These switches caused me to grow, expand and move with less hesitation.

Well, so much for my comfort zone. Then again, at the end of my comfort zone new lives begin. How amazing is that?

Kingdom Takeaway

Think about the areas where you feel stretched. Have you been stagnating lately? Are things just not as exciting as they were in the beginning? Perhaps He's been calling you to step out. What are some ways you can step into *His* comfort zone and out of your *own*?

Shift. Become more flexible. Even if you're afraid of the unknown, consider it an adventure of discovery—a discovery of his mysteries.

Be like Gumby—*flexible.*

One Blessing More

By JoAnne Meckstroth

If we are to better the future we must disturb the present.

—Catherine Booth

The young girl kicked up a plume of dust, skipping quickly after her family as they wandered through the desert. Her family did not worry. They knew she was near by the ever-present tinkle and jingle of her many bangles and ankle bracelets.

"Achsah!" her mother called. She shook her head as her daughter laughed and bounced away, determined to make her own path in the dusty ground. She and Caleb had named their daughter Achsah (Hebrew for "anklet") because they had finally had a daughter and she was going to be spoiled with appropriate girly things.

While Achsah was as feminine as her mother, she most certainly had her father's boldness and courage. Her mother sighed. She was definitely Caleb's daughter. Continuing to move with the group, she kept a watchful eye on Achsah. The girl was bound to get into mischief along the way.

On cool desert nights, Achsah often snuggled close to her father as the family gathered around the crackling campfire. Attentive faces glimmered in the flickering light as they listened to Caleb's stories of slaying giants and living in the Promised Land. The tension and excitement were tangible as he described the provisions this land would supply the family. This, he declared to the collective sighs of his audience, is where they would dwell—in the fertile land surrounding Hebron, a land promised him by Moses many years earlier (Joshua 14:8–15).

Dreaming out loud, Caleb went on to detail the kinds of scrumptious food they'd be tasting—plump dates, juicy grapes, green vegetables and sweet honey. Their mouths watered.

Many of them knew nothing but the manna God had provided daily for them on their wilderness trek. Achsah tried to imagine the sensation of biting into something called a grape and having its juice burst in her mouth. It was almost too much to comprehend, but she listened intently and dreamed big with him.

A Prize for the Taking

After forty long years, Israel was coming out of the desert. Moses was no longer with them, but Joshua had taken his place as leader. Those whose fear had delayed their entry into the Promised Land were long dead in the wilderness. Joshua and Caleb knew forty years ago just how ripe the land was for the taking. Now they finally had the chance to do battle with its giants and forcibly pull down their strongholds.

Once they'd established a toehold in the land, Joshua divided it into parcels for each tribe to claim. With that completed, Caleb and his troops wasted no time taking Hebron and slaying the giants who'd held it (Joshua 14:6–15). Satisfied with his conquest, he turned his attention to Debir, a city some fifteen or so miles to the south. He had a plan for that land and Achsah was on his mind.

Caleb wanted a strong husband for his daughter—one capable of matching her bold and fearless personality. He offered her hand in marriage to any man in the tribe willing to slay the last of the giants and conquer Debir with him. This city was the center of Canaanite culture. It's where the educators and scribes lived. Caleb knew that in order to change the culture, he had to conquer this last piece of land. His younger brother's son Othniel, stepped up to the challenge and won Achsah as his bride prize. Her father gave a piece of land as her dowry—an unusual gift for a young woman of that day. But Caleb knew that Promised Land acreage was worth far more than jewels and coins. (Joshua 15:13–19)

Delighted yet saddened, Caleb and his wife watched their only daughter leave home to live with her new husband. How would they fare in this new culture? It was a time of transition for Israel. Their nomadic lives were changing into agricultural ones. With that came new values, new government and new culture. Would they be godly leaders in these changing times?

Something More

When Achsah surveyed the dowry land given to her and Othniel, she realized it was arid and dry. Without water, neither vegetation nor any agricultural endeavor could survive, much less thrive. She needed more, so she saddled her donkey and returned to her father.

Caleb chuckled as he watched the distant figures grow larger. He was not surprised as Achsah's entourage approached. He knew his audacious daughter well and assumed she wanted something more.

Catching sight of Caleb from a distance, she dismounted, a sign of her enduring respect. "What can I do for you?" he asked.

"Father, you gave us a parcel of land, and for that we are very grateful," she began, "but there is no water. Please give me one blessing more—springs of water."

Caleb was unable to deny his daughter's request and was proud of her boldness in the asking. He added an adjoining field to her dowry, one which contained both upper and lower springs, virtually ensuring the productivity of her land (Joshua 15:18–19).

As the newly-married couple returned home, they were secure in the knowledge that their household would be fed, their potential for commerce improved and their worth would increase—all because she dared to ask for more.

Achsah and Us

I believe Achsah's story has a lot to say to us. Our heavenly Father wants us to take ground for his kingdom just as Caleb did. He wants to give us land, authority and provision. He wants us to help take down the giants in the high places occupied by Satan in our own land the way Othniel helped Achsah's father slay the giants of Debir. Through us, God will dethrone and destroy the works of the enemy and replace his kingdom with God's kingdom (Colossians 2:15). Some will have key leadership roles in society, bringing cultural change over regions, states and nations. Many of us will do this one soul at a time—through the unglamorous and little-publicized life of compassion, mercy and small things.

Achsah asked big and lived big. She asked for more land with springs of water.

Like her, we must ask our Father for more—more springs of living water flowing onto our land, releasing fruitfulness into everything we occupy and do (John 7:37–39). Then we'll have the privilege of leaving a rich and lasting inheritance for many generations.

Achsah and her family brought godly principles into their culture and Jesus brought heaven with Him wherever He went. We can do the same and demonstrate the supernatural power of the Spirit and share godly values that inspire people in how they think, live and see the world.

Expanding the Kingdom

Achsah's identity was not limited to being a good daughter. She became a land baron, a businesswoman, an influencer and a unifier in her society. Under her leadership, the two springs of water became a destination for the tired and thirsty sojourners traveling through the desert, a place where they replenished supplies in the marketplace and rested awhile.

Her bridegroom Othniel was not only a mighty warrior—he became the first of sixteen judges over Israel. When the Babylonians raided Hebron and the surrounding area, he gathered together a mighty army and defeated the king and delivered the land. For the next forty years, under Othniel's leadership, the people lived in peace and rest (Judges 3: 9-11).

These two powerful leaders were instrumental in changing and expanding the culture of the kingdom of God.

Our Bridegroom is a conqueror, too—Jesus conquered Satan, death, hell and the grave. Like Othniel, He's paid the bride price for us and defeated every foe. He not only reigns over Israel, He's also king of the kingdom. We, too, are expanding our Bridegroom's kingdom through the practical application of the Word of God and guidance of Holy Spirit.

Generational Provision

Several years ago, I traveled with Lana Heightley on a trip to Israel. Standing on Achsah's inherited land, we marveled at God's generational provision.

The springs are still there, witnessing to God's faithfulness to a believing, faith-filled woman. To this day, the land remains an important commercial and agricultural area in Israel.

For a moment, our thoughts went back in time to stand with this bold, fearless woman. We dreamed big and asked big. We declared that rivers of living water would flow in and out of us into the nations of the world, where godly principles would flow freely and sustain future generations.

Kingdom Takeaway

How about you? Are you free to dream big or have you lost sight of your purpose and future? This is the time for you to draw near to Him and believe for new revelation and insight into your destiny. New springs flow from the base of His throne, ready to overflow into the land He has given you.

Through Achsah's story, we see the results of the Scripture in Matthew 7:7–8. "Ask and it will be given to you; seek and you will find; knock and the door will be opened to you. For everyone who asks receives; he who seeks finds; and to him who knocks, the door will be opened," (NKJV).

So why not ask big? By faith, keep seeking until God opens the door to your request. God, like Caleb, is willing to work on your behalf. He desires to use you for His glory—to equip you as an influencer in His kingdom. And some day—just maybe—future generations will be inspired to dream big, live big and ask big from God because of the inheritance you have left behind.

Up for the Challenge

By JoAnne Meckstroth

Build history with God and He will build history through you.

—Bill Johnson

When did we start thinking God wants to send us to safe places to do easy things? Jesus didn't die to keep us safe. He died to make us dangerous—to make us a prophetic gateway which reveals His thoughts, His unwavering authority and His heart of unconditional love. To make us so completely fearless in our faith that when Satan sees us coming, he cries out, "Oh no! Here comes trouble."

History is filled with dangerous men and women who have packed up courage and taken heaven's story to familiar and not so familiar places. People who have stepped out in faith and followed God's call—to go where they've never gone and to do what they've never done. People who have lived a life worth telling stories about.

Now *This* is a Story Worth Telling

Let me tell you about Caleb, the less celebrated friend of Joshua. He was not only dangerous—he was a giant slayer, a kingdom-builder and a man after God's own heart. Because of his tenacity and fearless nature, Moses chose him as one of the twelve spies sent on the famous reconnaissance mission in Numbers 13 to check out the Promised Land. He was up for the challenge.

All the spies saw the huge giants living in the land God wanted to give Israel, but neither Caleb nor Joshua allowed this threat to rattle them. They compared the giants to the Almighty God and brought back a positive report. "Moses, this land is big and bountiful. The soil is rich for planting, the livestock are producing milk by the gallons and the bees are making honey faster than the gentiles can eat it. Taste these delicious grapes we brought back to you! Yes, there are giants twice our size, but we can do this. God is with us."

The other ten spies saw things differently—they compared the giants to themselves. "We are like grasshoppers next to those giants. We'll never win. They'll kill us all." Despite the power and miracles God had shown during their release from slavery, the Israelites still didn't get it. They begged Moses to turn back to Egypt, preferring the safety of what was familiar (slavery) to the fear of unknown dangers they'd face by seeking freedom.

No matter how loudly the Israelites wailed, Moses was not about to take them backward. Instead, for the next forty years, he led the people, along with Caleb and Joshua, through the harsh, unforgiving desert where their beliefs, values and dreams were tested.

How about you? Have you been wandering in a personal desert, wondering what in the world God's purpose is in your struggle? If you are currently facing a situation that seems beyond your strength or understanding, take time to rehearse your history with the Lord and you just may come out with a plan—maybe even a battle plan—that will help you overcome your present situation.

Or maybe you've thought of the dry desert as a place of punishment. I guarantee He is not the sort of Father who intentionally brings torment or persecution into your life. And yet, He will do whatever is necessary to keep you away from a challenge you are not prepared to face, just as He did with the Israelites. To regain a godly perspective on your desert experience, answer this question: *Are my problems bigger than God, or is God bigger than my problem?*

Possibly, like Caleb, your desert wanderings have little to do with your choices, but you've fallen victim to circumstances outside of your control. God not only prepared him for this kind of conflict, but He led him right into it. Caleb didn't dwell on the fact the people's choices pushed against his dreams. Instead, he rose above his disappointment and focused on the superior reality that their choices could not cancel out his destiny.

Even though it took Caleb another forty years to enter Canaan, his desire to displace the enemy remained strong. He was as passionate about slaying giants in his eighties as he had been in his forties. In Joshua 14, when Joshua began to parcel out the land, there was old Caleb, waiting in line.

He must have looked out of place amongst the buff, muscular young men in his tribe—his leathered face etched with deep wrinkles and sun-parched, sagging skin.

But Caleb wasn't intimidated. Pounding his staff into the ground, he declared, "I'm as strong this day as on the day that Moses sent me to spy out the land. Just as my strength was then, so now is my strength for war. Now give me this mountain."

Caleb's Spirit Lives On

Peter Milne was a 20th century Caleb. In his day, a special breed of missionaries packed their belongings in a wooden coffin, waved goodbye to family, friends, and their pasts and traveled to dangerous and unknown parts of the world. They were described as "one-way missionaries."

Peter Milne was up for the challenge and became one of them. God called him to a tribe of headhunters in Nguna, New Hebrides. Even though all the other missionaries who'd ever visited this tribe had been martyred (not exactly a storybook ending), Milne didn't shrink back into *safe* Christianity. Like Caleb, he was determined to slay every cultural giant that stood in the way of his assignment.

To establish the kingdom of God on this little patch of land, he lived among them and saw them through God's eyes. He didn't fault their pagan culture and demand they adopt his. He didn't insist they cover their naked bodies and throw away their past as if it had no value. Had he done so, the locals would have cut off his head and hung it up to dry.

Instead, he did it God's way. Over the next forty plus years, Milne introduced the dynamic faith of Jesus Christ with such power and reality that when the people in the community experienced His love, their old ways simply fell away. According to Mike Batterson in his book *All In,* the tribe wrote the following words on his tombstone: *When he came there was no light. When he left there was no darkness.*

What an incredible inscription of someone's life. Milne introduced them to a holy existence that changed the way they thought, talked and lived.

What might our communities look like if we faced our cultural giants with the same "no turning back" attitude?

Caleb in a Skirt

While ministering on the island of Fiji with Dr. Janet Mangum, I was sent to teach in the local villages and churches. On one such occasion, the atmosphere was filled with His presence and the power of the Holy Spirit flowed freely among us. As people stepped onto the mountain of faith, they were healed, delivered and filled anew with God's love. Upon saying goodbye to the congregation, the young pastor slipped a piece of paper into my hand. On it was scrawled this note. "Pastor JoAnne, I see the spirit of Caleb upon you. Just as he carried a different spirit, so do you. You are a dangerous woman—a giant slayer. Just as Caleb conquered mountains in his old age, so shall you."

This prophetic word not only gave me a glimpse of God's heart for me, but it pulled me into another dimension of His call and anointing. Although I had slayed a few giants in my day, I wasn't sure I had enough faith and determination to steward this prophetic promise to the end like Caleb had. Or would I fall back into second-guessing? *Was this prophecy really from God or was this man just a "wannabe" prophet?*

Arriving back at the mission house, I dropped to my knees in prayer. "Lord, was this prophecy really inspired by You? If this is true, what do I have to do?"

During our intimate exchange, I heard the familiar words, "JoAnne, just be." In other words, "Relax. Don't overthink it. I've got this." The Lord had often used these words to calm down my anxiety and bring clarity to whatever circumstances I was going through. Instantly, I knew God had already started weaving Caleb's spirit into mine.

Even with God's help, fulfilling this prophecy was not going to be easy. I knew who I was *not* and would not have compared myself to Caleb. But I was up for the challenge.

I knew I was different. My family thought I was crazy. And I was—crazy in love with Jesus. My religious friends called me foolish because my radical faith didn't fit into their traditional mold. My secular friends shook their heads and called me a Jesus fanatic.

However, I don't think this was the "different spirit" God was talking about.

Heaven's Hero

Numbers 14:24 says Caleb had *another* spirit. He was divinely connected and inspired by the Holy Spirit. Deep trust and unconditional love was the centerpiece of their relationship. He was known to be a man of faith, obedience and courage. When he heard from God, he set his face like flint and never looked back.

Caleb was heaven's hero. He exemplified his name—wholehearted, brave and faithful. He understood kingdom authority and knew what to do with it. His mind didn't yield to the world's way of thinking. He didn't doubt God's greatness, nor did he fear the giants. This "one-way missionary" was kingdom-minded and kingdom-motivated to the core. After forty plus years, he still had the raging confidence to establish the kingdom of God in Hebron. Along with Peter Milne, Caleb understood that cultures don't die—they must be exchanged.

The Great Exchange

Once Caleb plundered hell and slayed the giants, God shifted his focus and deployed him as a kingdom-infused leader. It was no longer about Caleb the warrior slaying giants and conquering mountains. It was now about a compassionate and wise man leading the people living on the mountain. God looked beyond Caleb's external circumstances and awakened the powerful leader within him.

By faith, Caleb led the Canaanites into a new way of thinking, behaving and living—replacing their wicked ways with the superior ways of God's kingdom, a culture that honored God as "Lord of all the earth," where His voice was heard and followed among the affairs of men. A kingdom culture was born all because Caleb was up for the challenge.

Kingdom Takeaway

How about you? Just as Caleb and Joshua, Peter Milne and I were willing to fight the giants on our land, you must be prepared to take down a few yourself. Moses isn't here to hold you back. You don't have to wait forty-plus years to dwell on your piece of land.

His kingdom doesn't rest only on the shoulders of well-known leaders but on those with "another spirit"—whose actions speak louder than words and whose radical confidence in God releases supernatural power. Jesus wasn't kidding in Luke 24:49 when he told the disciples not to leave home without the Holy Spirit.

Be dangerous. Be willing to do whatever, whenever, wherever God calls you. Know who God says you are. Be a flashing light in the dark shadows of today's culture, where reasoning is often short-circuited, and emotionalism has surged to an explosive crescendo. Be ready with a life-giving, relevant word when the opportunity is given. God has wired you uniquely for this battle.

Will you get in line with me and boldly ask for more land to conquer, more giants to slay, and more of God's kingdom to establish? Yes, the cultural giants are huge and dangerous. But they are but insects when looking through God's eyes.

This is what you and I are born *again* for. To establish God's kingdom culture once again in the messy, chaotic world of the 21st century.

Besieged, Bothered and Bewildered

By Sue Chamberlain

This day is a day of good news. . .Now therefore, come, let us go and tell.

(2 Kings 7:9 NKJV)

Besieged, bothered and bewildered. Sounds like today's headlines, doesn't it? We've been besieged by an unknown virus, bothered by face masks and now bewildered at conflicting decisions coming from those in authority.

How does a citizen of God's kingdom get through all this? Reverend Kent Christmas once said, "The nature of God is revealed to Christians through chaos."

Second Kings 7:1 cautioned the Israelites to "Hear the Word of the Lord." It's still good advice today. How does the Lord speak to us by His Holy Spirit? He communicates to us through His Word, His ministers, and through nature. The question is: what are we doing with that Word when we hear it?

Elisha's Story

In 2 Kings, the army of Aram laid siege to a city in Samaria. The siege had gone on so long that, "a donkey's head sold for eighty shekels of silver, and a quarter of a cab of seed pods for five shekels," (2 Kings 6:25 NKJV). In other words, the people were starving.

At last, God spoke to them through the prophet Elisha, promising a supernatural miracle before twenty-four hours had passed. How did those in authority receive this word? With skepticism and unbelief. "Look, even if the Lord should open the floodgates of the heavens, could this happen?" (2 Kings 7:2 NKJV)

The officer who spoke these words had forgotten the promise was coming from the same God who in one day had parted the Red Sea to deliver Israel from Egypt. He was the same God who in one day had brought down the walls of Jericho.

But God's timing was perfect! When He said, "about this time tomorrow," it was because He'd already set a strategy in motion to bring it about.

Four unlikely men appeared in 2 Kings 7:3–4. Lepers outside the city gate were about to become part of God's strategy. Like those inside, these four were starving. Basically, they asked each other, "Why are we sitting here until we die? Let's go over to the enemy's camp and surrender. They may spare us. But, hey, we're going to die, anyway."

Before the lepers rose for the journey, God was already putting His plan in motion. He caused the army of Aram to hear the noise of chariots and horses. They thought they were being attacked and fled the camp, leaving behind horses, tents, food, silver, gold and clothing.

The men who had left the city gates feeling as if they had nothing to lose found a camp emptied of enemies when they got there. Bewildered and beside themselves, they sat down to eat and drink before hiding the silver, gold and clothes.

That's where the story could have ended, but God was still at work. They came to themselves, saying, "We are not doing right. This day is a day of good news, and we remain silent. . .Now therefore, come, let us go and tell," (2 Kings 7:9 NKJV). Once the king settled his doubts and checked out their story, he found food aplenty and the city was saved!

A World Under Siege

Today the world is locked in like that city in Samaria. Besieged with smart phones, laptops, and computer games, many are starving for the Bread of Life. Without some breakthrough, they will die.

Some unbelievers remain doubtful—even cynical—like the people in the story. As Christians, we may feel like lepers, outcast from the world's values. Yet here we are, sitting outside the city with the riches of Christ piled around us.

The world may not believe us. They may not believe the gospel, the second coming of Christ, or even the judgment, but we cannot hoard the Good News. We cannot remain silent. We must go and tell others.

I want to be part of ending the spiritual famine today. How about you? Then let's be bold and share the Good News!

Kingdom Takeaway

Be the one who shares the Good News. Don't wait for someone else when God is ready to empower *you*.

Just as the four men rose out of their silence, so must our voice resonate the kingdom story. God is looking for faith-filled people who will not bow to fear, discouragement or self-centeredness. He is saying, "I am with you! Let's go!"

A Final Word

Now that you've read the chronicles of these fourteen women, what did you notice about them?

These are ordinary people facing circumstances any of us may encounter. Some are in full-time ministry, while others serve nine-to-five in a workplace or work twenty-four-seven at home. What binds them together is a shared citizenship in a most extraordinary kingdom.

The resources of courage and spiritual authority these women drew on came from the spiritual home in which they live—God's dwelling place. While some of their backgrounds or experiences may have impressed you, we hope you noticed it wasn't their outward qualifications that brought them success but their connection with God's Holy Spirit.

We trust these stories have brought you hope—hope that, by the power and provision of the Holy Spirit, you can become greater than you ever imagined as your relationship with the Lord Jesus grows increasingly deeper.

You don't need to be extraordinary by human standards to have your own tales of guts, glory and kingdom authority. The Apostle Paul encourages us not to be over-awed by others. "Think of what you were when you were called. Not many of you were wise by human standards; not many were influential; not many were of noble birth. But God chose the foolish things of the world to shame the wise; God chose the weak things of the world to shame the strong. . .so that no one may boast before him. . .Therefore, as it is written: 'Let him who boasts boast in the Lord,'" (1 Corinthians 1:26–31 NIV).

So, even if you feel no better than one of those "foolish things" about whom Paul spoke, take heart. You can become a living kingdom chronicle—one whose story brings glory to God. Put your hand in the hand of Jesus the Christ and let Him escort you into His kingdom. Then draw your strength from Him.

Authors

Melanie Boudreau

Melanie Boudreau is an ordained minister and author and founder of Relationship Restoration Strategies, created to increase quality of life for children with autism and their caregivers in nations or regions with little access to effective interventions. (RRSautism.org)

She wrote *Toppling the Idol of Ideal: Raising Children with Hidden Disabilities* and is currently working to shift the trajectory of autism intervention for nations in need of an effective, affordable model independent of heavy medical infrastructure.

For blogging and further contact information: melanieboudreau.com

Sue Chamberlain

Sue Chamberlain has been a Bible teacher for sixty years and is former owner of a Christian bookstore for twenty-five years. She has been a tourism consultant for trips to the Holy Land and attended the Institute for Holy Land studies in Jerusalem.

She is a team member for WWAM trips and author of *SonShine Segments from Sue* available from Amazon.

Renee Duncan

Renee Duncan is a global influencer. She produces and directs multiple international Christian weekly TV programs to reach people of all ages and faiths to reveal Christ. She has forty years of pastoral ministry alongside her husband. She is a keynote speaker and has held positions in multiple state and local leadership in the secular and Christian world.

She mentors leaders around the world and is a key player in collaborating with multiple international ministries to accomplish sharing the Good News of Jesus Christ.

Contact: www.linkedin.com/in/ANeueNow and Aneuenow@gmail.com

Pamela Eichorn

Pamela Eichorn is the Regional Director for The Great Lakes Ohio Valley Region of Aglow International. This region covers the states of Ohio, Indiana, Kentucky and Michigan.

Pam is a leader of leaders who employs her maverick approach of "permission granted" to raise the possibilities for everyone around her. She has a unique style of insight combined with a no-nonsense manner that is refreshing. She has an uncanny ability to simplify problems and point out solutions utilizing the lost art of common sense.

Pam co-authored the book *Uniquely His* and is currently working on a book of her own. Pam owns a small publishing company, Ajoyin Publishing. She is a graduate of Liberty University with an MBA in International Business.

You can contact her at: Ajoyin2014@gmail.com

Frances (Fran) Hallgren

Frances Hallgren is a worshiping evangelist. Double degreed in Music Education and Theology, she currently teaches seminars on Worship and Music Ministry and serves as the Assistant Director for the Transformation Department of Aglow International, taking short-term mission teams all over the world as well as bringing them to her own back yard—Alaska.

Contact email: frantastic@fastimap.com

Lana Heightley

Lana Heightley is the founder and President of Women With A Mission (WWAM). As an ordained minister, she has worked in world missions for over 35 years. WWAM was first established for the empowering, training and equipping women. However, today all leaders are included, encouraging and releasing them into their destinies. Her peers refer to her as Dr. Lana Heightley, an apostle to the nations.

WWAM has worked in over 40 nations. Through these partnerships, over one million people have received the gospel and been trained for kingdom purposes as well as establishing and building churches in many of those nations. Her expertise and anointing enables her to aid leaders discover their gifts, talents, purpose and destiny awareness and fulfillment. She serves on several ministry boards, teaches Bible studies, serves as a counselor, and has worked in ministries including Aglow International, Ladies Missions Director and New Life Church. She is a member of International Coalition of Apostolic Leaders.

Her four books: *Presents from on High*, *Divine Assignments*, *Upshift* and *Glory Connections* are available on Amazon.

Valerie Johnson

Valerie (Val) Johnson was ordained in1995. She worked as an apostolic liaison with other ministers launching churches, holding tent meetings and preaching the gospel, and as a visionary with a prophetic call to help the bound be set free from spiritual darkness.

She is the founder of InGod2win, a 22-year-old prayer ministry that conducts health and healing summits with weekly prayer meetings.

She is a volunteer at her local church as a teacher/intercessor and serves as President for Aglow International Southfield.

Contact: www.InGod2win.org

Melonie Janet Mangum

Melonie Janet Mangum is an ordained minister with two doctorate degrees in theology. As a past special education teacher, she led support groups for parents of children with special needs. Since 1993, she has worked with outreach teams of all ages and ethnicities. She is the founder and president of Partners for Transformation, serving currently as Director of Transformation in Aglow International.

She is the author of six books available on Amazon.

Contact email:melonie.mangum@me.com

Merrily Madero

Merrily Madero is an Assemblies of God Ordained Minister who splits her time between Michigan, Colorado and Quebec, Canada. Merrily is a retired Colonel who led military soldiers for thirty years in the US Air Force. She has a BS in Mechanical Engineering, a BA in Theology and three different MS degrees.

She is the founder and president of M3 International, where she is called on to preach and teach many leadership and ministry courses throughout the USA and around the world. Her latest book, *The Truth About Consequences*, is available on her website or Amazon.

Contact: MerrilyMadero@gmail.com or www.M3international.org.

JoAnne Meckstroth

JoAnne Meckstroth is a writer, inspirational speaker, leadership trainer, consultant, mentor and founder of Women of Impact Ministries. She has served in key leadership roles in the Body of Christ for over 35 years in both the United States and internationally. She is the former Northwest Regional Director for Aglow International, former Executive Director of Care Net, Inc. Alaska and had a career in the business world for over 25 years. Living in Alaska for over 40 years, it is only natural that God would use her as a pioneer and groundbreaker.

She is passionate about raising up women of excellence in whatever role God has assigned them. Her gentle yet bold and interactive style of speaking, writing and training transcends the generations.

Contact JoAnne at: joanne.meckstroth@gmail.com

Lecia Retter

Lecia Retter is the founder and president of The Unstoppable Prayer Movement, a 24/7 prayer movement dedicated to the end of human trafficking (upmovement.org).

She directs a prayer network at a local university and is a professional intercessor.

Contact email: info@upmovement.org

Rosemarie Waters

Rosemarie Waters has served as Director of Women's Ministry in her church. She is a businesswoman, an entrepreneur and passionate student of the Word of God.

As an inspirational speaker, she enjoys sharing God's redemption story and fanning the flames of others.

Contact email: akrose18@gmail.com

Sarah Williams

Sarah Williams, an ordained minister, is currently Founder and President of Northwest Women of Valor, an organization to embolden and challenge women to arise as Victorious Warriors. She has served in many leadership capacities in ministry as teacher, trainer and encourager.

She also has been a successful businesswoman for many years.

Made in the USA
Monee, IL
15 May 2022